10/18/15
$24.95

Reality
Therapy

Theories of Psychotherapy Series

Theories of Psychotherapy Series
Jon Carlson and Matt Englar-Carlson, Series Editors

Reality Therapy

Robert E. Wubbolding

American Psychological Association

Washington, DC

Published by
American Psychological Association
750 First Street, NE
Washington, DC 20002
www.apa.org

To order
APA Order Department
P.O. Box 92984
Washington, DC 20090-2984
Tel: (800) 374-2721;
Direct: (202) 336-5510
Fax: (202) 336-5502;
TDD/TTY: (202) 336-6123
Online: www.apa.org/books/
E-mail: order@apa.org

In the U.K., Europe, Africa, and the
Middle East, copies may be ordered from
American Psychological Association
3 Henrietta Street
Covent Garden, London
WC2E 8LU England

Typeset in Minion by Shepherd, Inc., Dubuque, IA

Printer: United Book Press, Baltimore, MD
Cover Designer: Minker Design, Sarasota, FL
Cover Art: *Lily Rising*, 2005, oil and mixed media on panel in craquelure frame, by Betsy Bauer

The opinions and statements published are the responsibility of the authors, and such opinions and statements do not necessarily represent the policies of the American Psychological Association.

Library of Congress Cataloging-in-Publication Data

Wubbolding, Robert E.
   Reality therapy / Robert E. Wubbolding. — 1st ed.
       p. ; cm. — (Theories of psychotherapy series)
   Includes bibliographical references and index.
   ISBN-13: 978-1-4338-0853-1
   ISBN-10: 1-4338-0853-6
   ISBN-13: 978-1-4338-0854-8 (e-book)
   ISBN-10: 1-4338-0854-4 (e-book)
   1. Reality therapy. I. American Psychological Association. II. Title. III. Series: Theories of psychotherapy series.
   [DNLM: 1. Reality Therapy. WM 420 W959r 2011]
   RC489.R37W826 2011
   616.89'165—dc22
                                   2010019769

British Library Cataloguing-in-Publication Data
A CIP record is available from the British Library.

Printed in the United States of America
First Edition

Contents

Series Preface

Some might argue that in the contemporary clinical practice of psychotherapy, evidence-based intervention and effective outcome have overshadowed theory in importance. Maybe. But, as the editors of this series, we don't propose to take up that controversy here. We do know that psychotherapists adopt and practice according to one theory or another because their experience, and decades of good evidence, suggests that having a sound theory of psychotherapy leads to greater therapeutic success. Still, the role of theory in the helping process can be hard to explain. This narrative about solving problems helps convey theory's importance:

> Aesop tells the fable of the sun and wind having a contest to decide who was the most powerful. From above the earth, they spotted a man walking down the street, and the wind said that he bet he could get his coat off. The sun agreed to the contest. The wind blew and the man held on tightly to his coat. The more the wind blew, the tighter he held. The sun said it was his turn. He put all of his energy into creating warm sunshine and soon the man took off his coat.

What does a competition between the sun and the wind to remove a man's coat have to do with theories of psychotherapy? We think this deceptively simple story highlights the importance of theory as the precursor to any effective intervention—and hence to a favorable outcome. Without a guiding theory, we might treat the symptom without understanding the role of the individual. Or we might create power conflicts with our clients and not understand that, at times, indirect means of helping (sunshine) are often as effective—if not more so—than direct ones (wind). In the absence of theory, we might lose track of the treatment rationale and instead get caught up in, for example, social correctness and not wanting to do something that looks too simple.

What exactly *is* theory? The *APA Dictionary of Psychology* defines theory as "a principle or body of interrelated principles that purports to explain or predict a number of interrelated phenomena." In psychotherapy, a theory is a set of principles used to explain human thought and behavior, including what causes people to change. In practice, a theory creates the goals of therapy and specifies how to pursue them. Haley (1997) noted that a theory of psychotherapy ought to be simple enough for the average therapist to understand but comprehensive enough to account for a wide range of eventualities. Furthermore, a theory guides action toward successful outcomes while generating hope in both the therapist and client that recovery is possible.

Theory is the compass that allows psychotherapists to navigate the vast territory of clinical practice. In the same ways that navigational tools have been modified to adapt to advances in thinking and ever-expanding territories to explore, theories of psychotherapy have changed over time. The different schools of theories are commonly referred to as waves, the first wave being psychodynamic theories (i.e., Adlerian, psychoanalytic), the second wave learning theories (i.e., behavioral, cognitive–behavioral), the third wave humanistic theories (person-centered, gestalt, existential), the fourth wave feminist and multicultural theories, and the fifth wave postmodern and constructivist theories. In many ways, these waves represent how psychotherapy has adapted and responded to changes in psychology, society, and epistemology as well as to changes in the nature of psychotherapy itself. Psychotherapy and the theories that guide it are dynamic and responsive. The wide variety of theories is also testament to the different ways in which the same human behavior can be conceptualized (Frew & Spiegler, 2008).

It is with these two concepts in mind—the central importance of theory and the natural evolution of theoretical thinking—that we developed the APA Theories of Psychotherapy Series. Both of us are thoroughly fascinated by theory and the range of complex ideas that drive each model. As university faculty members who teach courses on the theories of psychotherapy, we wanted to create learning materials that not only highlight the essence of the major theories for professionals and professionals in training but also clearly bring the reader up to date on the current status of the models. Often in books on theory, the biography of the original theorist overshadows the evolution of the model. In contrast, our intent is to highlight the contemporary uses of the theories as well as their history and context.

As this project began, we faced two immediate decisions: which theories to address and who best to present them. We looked at graduate-level theories of psychotherapy courses to see which theories are being taught, and we explored popular scholarly books, articles, and conferences to determine which theories draw the most interest. We then developed a dream list of authors from among the best minds in contemporary theoretical practice. Each author is one of the leading proponents of that approach as well as a knowledgeable practitioner. We asked each author to review the core constructs of the theory, bring the theory into the modern sphere of clinical practice by looking at it through a context of evidence-based practice, and clearly illustrate how the theory looks in action.

There are 24 titles planned for the series. Each title can stand alone or can be put together with a few other titles to create materials for a course in psychotherapy theories. This option allows instructors to create a course featuring the approaches they believe are the most salient today. To support this end, APA Books has also developed a DVD for each of the approaches that demonstrates the theory in practice with a real client. Many of the DVDs show therapy over six sessions. Contact APA Books for a complete list of available DVD programs (http://www.apa.org/pubs/videos).

William Glasser's reality therapy (based on choice theory) is a popular approach in contemporary therapy. This approach focuses on the immediate or here-and-now world of the client and how clients' current actions move them closer or further away from their stated goals. In *Reality Therapy*, Glasser's main protégé, Robert E. Wubbolding, highlights the practical commonsense nature of this approach by providing illustrative case examples that depict this model in action. Further, the history of how Glasser developed this approach in response to clinical dilemmas highlights the practical and direct application of the model. Readers will quickly understand the importance of problem solving and choice making and see why this approach has had such appeal in schools and community mental health centers.

—Jon Carlson and Matt Englar-Carlson

REFERENCES

Frew, J., & Spiegler, M. (2008). *Contemporary psychotherapies for a diverse world.* Boston, MA: Lahaska Press.

Haley, J. (1997). *Leaving home: The therapy of disturbed young people.* New York, NY: Routledge.

How to Use This Book With APA Psychotherapy Videos

Each book in the Theories of Psychotherapy Series is specifically paired with a DVD that demonstrates the theory applied in actual therapy with a real client. Many DVDs feature the author of the book as the guest therapist, allowing students to see an eminent scholar and practitioner putting the theory he or she writes about into action.

The DVDs have a number of features that make them excellent tools for learning more about theoretical concepts:

- Many DVDs contain six full sessions of psychotherapy over time, giving viewers a chance to see how clients respond to the application of the theory over the course of several sessions.
- Each DVD has a brief introductory discussion recapping the basic features of the theory behind the approach demonstrated. This allows viewers to review the key aspects of the approach about which they have just read.
- DVDs feature actual clients in unedited psychotherapy sessions. This provides a unique opportunity to get a sense of the look and feel of real psychotherapy, something that written case examples and transcripts cannot always convey.
- There is a therapist commentary track that viewers may choose to play during the psychotherapy sessions. This track gives unique insight into why therapists do what they do in a session. Further, it provides an in vivo opportunity to see how the therapist uses the model to conceptualize the client.

The books and DVDs together make a powerful teaching tool for showing how theoretical principles affect practice. In the case of this book, the DVD *Reality Therapy*, which features the author as the guest expert, provides a vivid example of how this approach looks in practice.

Acknowledgments

First and foremost I am indebted to William Glasser, MD, who founded reality therapy and has taught it for almost 5 decades. Throughout these years he has maintained and increased his unswerving commitment and unshakable belief that this system of counseling and therapy, as well as its other applications to education and all human relationships, is an inestimable force for improving societies and cultures around the world. Behavioral change is the focus of *reality therapy*, a term Dr. Glasser coined while working with mental patients and residents of a correctional institution. I am also indebted to Carleen, his wife, a teacher in her own right who steadfastly supports his every effort. I am proud to have introduced Bill and Carleen to each other.

Linda Harshman, executive director of The William Glasser Institute, has provided a steady hand guiding the organization for more than 25 years. She has been a friend and colleague whose constant support for both Dr. Glasser and me has been integral to the development of choice theory and reality therapy around the world.

I wish to express deep gratitude to Jon Carlson for his belief in the quality of my work and his willingness to involve me in his work. Thanks also to Ed Meidenbauer, whose editorial fine-tooth comb is among the best.

Although they were unaware of the help they have provided, my students, workshop participants, and clients have taught me the art of counseling and psychotherapy. I wish them the best as they plan for their futures.

Finally, my wife, Sandie, has been indispensable in her patient, loyal support and editing and reediting efforts. This book has been an exciting and fruitful occasion for enriching our life together.

My wish for all of the above is *ad multos annos*. A long and happy life.

Reality
Therapy

1

Introduction

"What do you want?" This question encapsulates a concept central to the practice of reality therapy and also provides a starting point to learn it. Many therapists consume valuable therapeutic hours without focusing on what clients want from the therapeutic process and from the world around them. Asking this question initiates the therapeutic relationship and strengthens it when clients and therapists make themselves available to the wealth of information contained in the myriad of wants, hopes, and dreams expressed through this simple but powerful question.

If you, the reader, ask yourself, "What do I want to gain from this book?" you will put yourself in the role of an eager student predisposed to maximum learning. Similarly, if you encounter a client who says he or she feels isolated, alienated, and without purpose, the first series of questions from the reality therapy point of view include: "What would you like to accomplish from our sessions together? Would you be interested in replacing this sense of alienation with something better, such as feelings of connectedness with others? Do you want to identify and pursue a life purpose?"

A careful reading of this book will result in a thorough understanding of the theory underlying reality therapy and its methodology while providing a seminal resource for both neophyte and experienced therapists.

Throughout the book I have emphasized the rationale behind reality therapy. Understanding the foundational principles helps practitioners avoid the perception that reality therapy and therapy in general can be reduced to overly simplified techniques. Reality therapy is practical and immediately useful to therapists seeking to enrich and broaden their skills. Nevertheless, understanding the theory and rationale for it enables therapists to develop their own individualized applications, skills, and techniques. For instance, asking clients the initial question "What do you want?" is an effective technique. It is also a concept, a principle inextricably connected to the theoretical principles of internal control psychology—that is, that human motivation is internal, a principle fully explained in this Introduction.

By focusing on reality and conscious issues rather than on the unconscious, William Glasser, MD (1965), the founder of reality therapy, challenged the assumptions and practice of the psychotherapeutic community. Assuming the ability of mental hospital patients to make choices and take responsibility for their behavior resulted in his professional marginalization. Undaunted by rejection, he forged ahead. This book explains a 21st-century system based on principles now widely accepted in the helping professions, that is internal control psychology.

These pages focus on two major and inseparable components: choice theory and reality therapy. Choice theory explains how the human mind functions as a negative input control system. A rocket is an example of such a system. When its aiming device signals that it is off target, it sends a message to its propulsion system to correct the difference between its current direction and its intended direction. Similarly, when the driver of a car sets the cruise control at a desired speed, the speed mechanism corrects the car's velocity when it detects a discrepancy between the current speed and the desired speed. Likewise, when human beings perceive that they are not getting what they want, this discrepancy causes the activation of their behavioral system; that is, they make corrective choices designed to keep them on target. On the other hand, when human beings perceive they are getting what they want from the world around them, they are satisfied. They are in a condition of homeostasis. Therefore, human behavior is purposeful. It is an attempt to influence the external world and to communicate with it. The goal of this effort is to gain specific perceptions that needs and wants are satisfied (Glasser 1980, 1984, 1998).

Reality therapy is best seen as rooted in this theory but has its own identity with clearly defined procedures. If choice theory is the track, reality therapy is the train that delivers the product. From its beginnings in a mental hospital and a correctional institution, it has now been applied to psychotherapy, education, management, and supervision as well as parenting and a range of other human relationships. As in many psychotherapy systems, the therapist first establishes a safe and friendly therapeutic atmosphere. The therapist then helps clients focus on current conscious issues by helping them define what they want from the world around them, examine the effectiveness of their choices, and make realistic plans for satisfying their wants and needs. A basic philosophical principle of reality therapy is that human beings are responsible for their behavior. Their external environment, early childhood experiences, and the impact of their cultural surroundings have played a major role in their development. Nevertheless, the reality therapist sees human beings as capable of alternative behavioral choices so that they need not remain victimized, trapped, or even haunted by these influences (Wubbolding, 2000a).

In learning reality therapy and in applying its principles, the acronym WDEP is an eminently useful tool. This system will be explained in later chapters in detail, but a brief orientation is in order. Each letter represents a cluster of concepts that together constitute the reality therapy procedures leading to change. W stands for asking clients what they want from the world around them. Included in this procedure is an exploration of how clients perceive themselves as well as the world around them. D represents the exploration of what clients are currently doing—that is, what behaviors they are exhibiting, including action, thinking, feeling, and physiology. The E signifies client self-evaluation, examining the effectiveness of behavior, the attainability of wants, and many other aspects of their motivation. The P denotes a plan of action leading toward desirable change.

It is clear that, strictly speaking, there is a difference between choice theory and reality therapy. On the other hand, in my teaching and lecturing, I often use the phrase *reality therapy* to encompass both theory and implementation—that is, choice theory and reality therapy. The reason is that reality therapy predates choice theory and the name William Glasser will always be connected to reality therapy. In conversations with university professors and practitioners, I have asked a simple question, "How will Dr. Glasser be remembered?" Almost to a person they respond that he will be remembered for founding reality therapy.

In learning reality therapy I encourage the reader to take special notice that the theory and practice of reality therapy are expressed in simple and clear language. I speak of belonging, power, freedom, fun, wants, choices, and perceptions. There is intentionally very little technical vocabulary, a fact that makes the system understandable to therapists and clients. In addition, I encourage the reader to select a specific person, perhaps the alienated and isolated client, the person feeling "put upon" by society, someone feeling dejected and depressed, someone acting out in an anti-social manner, or someone interested in his or her personal growth. As you learn each component of the theory and practice, ask yourself how the principles apply to this specific case.

2

History

ORIGIN

William Glasser, MD, shaped the seminal idea of reality therapy in a correctional institution and a psychiatric hospital in the 1950s and 1960s. Traditionally trained as a board-certified psychiatrist, Glasser learned the conventional methods of psychiatry: help clients gain insight, work through transference, deal with defense mechanisms, and thereby achieve a higher degree of adjustment and sanity. Through his experience with patients, however, he came to believe that in spite of achieving the goals of the analytic approach, clients often remained stuck in their ineffective behaviors, and many failed to take responsibility for their behavior and were ill-equipped to generate more effective choices. His professor, G. L. Harrington, provided support and a sympathetic ear enabling Glasser to formulate and implement the early principles of his new treatment modality later known as reality therapy. In 1960 Glasser published *Mental Health or Mental Illness* in which he presented the initial idea that mental health results from the satisfaction of internal needs. By satisfying internal motivators Glasser claimed, human beings are no longer victims trapped and oppressed by their environments.

The watershed year for reality therapy came in 1965, when Glasser published the controversial book *Reality Therapy: A New Approach to Psychiatry*. Contrary to the conventional wisdom of that time, Glasser emphasized that people who take responsibility for their own behavior and avoid placing blame on the past or on outside forces achieve a higher degree of mental health than those attributing their problems to parental influence, society, or their own past experiences. He asserted that behavior involves choices and that there are options available for most people in most circumstances. Consequently, the objective of counseling and psychotherapy should be measurable behavioral change, not merely insight into and understanding of past events or current unconscious drives.

Though not warmly received by the medical profession, corrections personnel, youth workers, psychologists, counselors, therapists, and educators welcomed reality therapy with its emphasis on personal responsibility. Glasser consulted in schools and helped students take charge of their behaviors and blame others less. Based on his experience in schools, he wrote the book *Schools Without Failure* (1968) in which he discussed class meetings or how to use reality therapy in large groups. While not the same as group counseling or psychotherapy, class meetings have some of the same goals, such as increased self-esteem, feelings of success, and group members' involvement with and respect for each other.

In the early days of reality therapy, many professionals viewed it not as a theory but only as a method. In developing an underlying theory, Glasser first formulated the sociological foundation in *The Identity Society* (1972). He explained that three forces had contributed to the radical changes in Western civilization in the 1950s and 1960s. During these decades Western society witnessed both gradual and sudden changes such as the passage of laws guaranteeing human rights, increased affluence satisfying the basic need for survival or self-preservation for the majority of people, and the onset of instant communication via electronic media. These three changes heralded the birth of the identity society, a world in which persons focus more on their identity needs than on their survival needs. Most people hope for and pursue opportunities for moving beyond economic and political serfdom. Therefore, because of its emphasis on personal empowerment by means of self-evaluation and positive planning for the future, reality therapy found approval by people seeking a higher level of inner control. This principle of holding people responsible for their behavior was the opposite of the psychotherapy theories of the 1960s. Yet, it has always been a principle by which people live and upon which a humane society rests. As Glasser and Zunin (1973) note:

> Reality therapy is one of the newest of man's formal attempts to explain mankind, to set rules for behavior, and to map out how one person can help another to achieve happiness and success; but at the same time, paradoxically, it represents one of the oldest sets of maxims referring to human conduct. (p. 287)

ANCIENT PRECURSOR

While some principles of choice theory are rooted in earlier psychologies, the foundations for internal control psychology and more specifically choice theory can be seen in ancient writings. As early as the second century, Marcus Aurelius, the Roman emperor (121–180 AD) spoke of personal responsibility in a world dominated by belief in external controls—that is, the whims of the pagan gods. Such statements as the following indicate the early philosophy of internal control:

> If anything is within the powers and province of man, believe that it is within your own compass also.
>
> The agitations that beset you are superfluous and depend wholly on judgments that are your own.
>
> Men's actions cannot agitate us but our own views regarding them [can stir human feelings].
>
> Today I got clear of trouble. Say rather, "Today I cleared trouble out." Trouble was not without, but within. (Aurelius, 1944)

RECENT PRECURSORS

A more recent intellectual ancestor was Paul Dubois, a Swiss physician, who lived in the early 1900s and who served his patients by helping them replace destructive cognition with more constructive thinking (Glasser & Zunin,

1973). The early reality therapy as practiced by Glasser and Harrington followed the psychology of William James, sometimes known as the father of American psychology, who believed that attitudes are changeable and therefore individuals can alter their lives by changing their attitudes. This perception of human beings as inwardly controlled, or internally motivated, is epitomized by James's famous axiom, "We do not sing because we are happy, we are happy because we sing." A more immediate foundation in the development of reality therapy was Helmut Kaiser, a psychoanalyst at the Menninger Foundation. He proposed, "It is the analyst's task to make the patient feel responsible for his own words and his own actions" (Kaiser, 1955/1965, p. 4). G. L. Harrington extended Kaiser's thinking with a more democratic doctor–patient relationship, which he believed promoted mental health more efficiently, thus deviating from the traditional theory and methodology that pervaded the psychoanalytic approach to mental health. In his lectures Glasser consistently referred to a woman he encountered as a psychiatric intern. She had spent 3 years in therapy discussing her grandfather and blaming him for her problems. Shortly after she became his client, Glasser learned the grandfather had died many years previously. He then set a boundary: They would talk only about current issues. In the next supervisory session with Harrington, Glasser described his insistence on the therapy focusing on current behavior and his deviation from conventional therapy. Rather than denying the validity of this approach, Harrington stated, "Join the club."

As a result of this significant conversation and their ongoing collegial relationship, Glasser gained the courage to develop specific procedures to be used in the practice of reality therapy to implement a fundamental unconventional principle: The behavior of human beings originates from within, springing from *current* motivational drives. After earning board certification as a qualified psychiatrist in 1961, Glasser began lecturing on "reality psychiatry," a label quickly changed to *reality therapy*. His psychiatric colleagues greeted the principles articulated with coldness and often with disdain. Yet, many other professionals desired more exposure to reality therapy and asked Glasser to provide a training program. Consequently, 2 years after publishing *Reality Therapy* (1965), he founded the Institute for Reality Therapy, now known as The William Glasser Institute, which continues to focus on training psychologists, counselors, social workers, educators, and an occasional psychiatrist (*Programs, Policies and Procedures of The William Glasser Institute*, 2005).

In 1965 Glasser developed his basic ideas when he became a consultant to the Ventura School, a California youth institution for delinquent girls under the leadership of Bea Dolan, Superintendent (1962–1976). The young female residents had broken the law and had frequently been told that because of their emotional disturbance, they were not responsible for their behavior. Dolan believed that such indoctrination served only to disempower the residents and wholeheartedly supported Glasser in his empathic but directive method of reality therapy. The use of reality therapy at the Ventura School for Girls provided an impetus for Glasser to further develop his ideas in future decades.

As interest in reality therapy increased, the sociological and anthropological foundations became evident (Glasser, 1972). Yet, this practical system lacked a justifying psychological theory. Control theory or control system theory provided the needed theoretical grounding. This relatively obscure explanation of brain functioning, little known in the helping professions but widely known in the fields of engineering and cybernetics, elevated reality therapy to the level of a free standing system. Control theory is a description of the human brain as a negative input control system. This means that human behavior is teleological or purposeful. When behavior does not achieve its intended purpose, the human brain receives negative feedback—that is, it perceives that behavior is off target and needs to be modified. Choice theory, the name Glasser later applied to control theory, provides an intricate explanation of the purpose and functions of human behavior, ability to make choices and perception as feedback.

NORBERT WIENER

Norbert Wiener (1894–1964) taught at MIT for 40 years and was beloved by his students as a brilliant and eccentric professor. He had earned a PhD from Harvard at age 18. In 1919 he worked for the General Electric Company in Lynn, Massachusetts; for Encyclopedia Americana in Albany, New York; at the Aberdeen Proving Grounds; and as a feature writer for the *Boston Herald*. His monumental work *Cybernetics* (1948), published the same year as George Orwell's *1984*, was less popular but far more prophetic. In both this work and in his later book *Nonlinear Problems in Random Theory* (1952), he initiated and developed his new approach to machines and people. If control theory is relatively unknown today, it was less accepted when first articulated by Wiener. In the 1961 revised edition of *Cybernetics,* he wrote, "the chief obstacles which I found in making my point were that the notions of . . . control theory were novel and perhaps even shocking to the established attitudes of the time" (p. 7).

He further applied the concept of feedback to neurophysiology, electrical engineering, medicine, "ultra rapid computing machines," and other phenomena. Because of the wide applicability of his work, Gregory Bateson and Margaret Mead asked him to devote his time and talent to anthropology and sociology. To their urgent entreaty Wiener responded,

> Much as I sympathize with their sense of urgency of the situation and as much as I hope that they and other competent workers will take up problems of this sort, I can share neither their feeling that this field has the first claim on my attention, nor their hopefulness that sufficient progress can be registered in this direction to have an appreciable therapeutic effect in the present diseases of society. (1948, p. 24)

On the contrary, his ideas have had an appreciable therapeutic effect, as Glasser has shown. Glasser has made Wiener's theory a clinical and educational model. Glasser's choice theory states that the purpose of behavior is to satisfy five human needs, explained below. When the human mind perceives that needs are unsatisfied, it signals the behavioral system to correct itself so that the purpose is more effectively fulfilled.

CONTEMPORARY APPROACH/ EVOLUTION TO PRESENT

William Powers

Other scholars have taken the torch of Norbert Wiener and carried it further. Students of cybernetics saw the human motivational implications in control theory. William Powers, computer expert and psychologist, provided more proximate groundwork for choice theory. His major work, *Behavior, the Control of Perception* (1973), presents the brain as an input control system similar to a thermostat that controls the temperature of a room. By analogy the thermostat perceives the room temperature at 80 degrees and desires it to be 72 degrees. It sends a signal to its behavioral system, the air conditioning unit, to do something, to take action, to generate a behavior—lower the room temperature. It then receives the input, the information it wants—that is, a perception of the room temperature at 72 degrees. Similarly, the cruise control of an automobile "wants" the car to travel at 60 miles per hour. When the outside world changes—when the road rises or falls in elevation, for example—the cruise control adjusts its behavior, resulting in the "perception" of traveling at the desired speed. Hence, the mind functions as a negative input control system. When a person is not proceeding toward his or her goal, the brain informs itself that the behavior is off target and attempts to correct it. Glasser (1980, 1984) extended Power's interpretation of control theory (or control system theory) by incorporating a system of needs or five genetic instructions—survival or self-preservation, love or belonging, power or inner control, freedom or independence, fun or enjoyment—which are the source of human behavior. They comprise the motivational engine driving and sustaining human choices. Glasser molded the theory to the clinical setting and the practice of counseling and psychotherapy. With the addition of these and many other ideas, it was no longer appropriate to call Glasser's theory control theory, and consequently the recognized name is now choice theory. Glasser (1996) states,

> I changed the name of control theory to choice theory because the word *control* implies strongly that it is a theory that controls people and this totally wrong implication is a turnoff. Choice theory is accurate and reflects what I have been teaching since 1961, which is *we choose all we do.* (p. 3)

In addressing the benefits learned from choice theory he added,

> Choice theory teaches that we are much more in control of our lives than we realize. Taking more effective control means making better

choices as you relate to everyone. You can learn through choice theory how people actually function: how we combine what is written in our genes with what we learn as we live our lives. (Glasser, 1998, p. 4)

Most recently, reality therapy is characterized by procedures leading to change. The WDEP acronym summarizes an array of possible interventions:

- W—exploring client wants, level of commitment, and perceived locus of control.
- D—exploring what the client is doing (i.e., total behavior).
- E—helping clients conduct self-evaluations of total behavior and wants.
- P—assisting clients to plan for the future (Glasser & Glasser, 2008; Wubbolding, 2000a).

In addition, Glasser has described mental health as a public educational issue. He sees choice theory and reality therapy as a most effective tool for community education leading to enhanced mental health. Therefore, reality therapy is a mental health system, not merely a system for remediating pathology (Glasser, 2005a).

Glasser Quality Schools represent a specific community intervention and application of reality therapy in education. Described as lead management rather than reality therapy, this application involves educators learning to help students gain a sense of internal satisfaction from learning, improve their behavior, and increase their academic achievement (Wubbolding, 2007).

THE DIFFERENCE BETWEEN CHOICE THEORY AND REALITY THERAPY

Individuals often ask, "What is the difference between choice theory and reality therapy?" *Webster's New World College Dictionary* (1999) defines theory as "a formulation of apparent relationships or underlying principles of certain observed phenomena . . . that branch of an art or science consisting of a knowledge of its principles and methods rather than in its practice" (p. 1485). *Merriam-Webster Online Dictionary* (2008) further states that the word *theory* includes "a belief, policy . . . proposed or followed as the basis of action . . . a plausible or scientifically acceptable principle or body of principles offered to explain phenomena." Choice theory provides an explanation of human behavior and how the human mind functions and thus serves as a basis for the delivery system reality therapy. The theory does not of itself include directives about how it should be implemented. Choice theory answers questions about why people do what they do, holding that people act from current internal motivations for the purpose of satisfying their human needs or genetic instructions. More specifically they seek to fulfill wants and resolve the difference between what they want and what they perceive they are attaining from the outer world (Glasser, 1980, 1998). According to Wubbolding and Brickell (2005), a second purpose of human behavior is to communicate, to send a message to people in the environment. They add,

> This message is often quite different from the one received by other people. For example, a rebellious adolescent wants to "be left alone" and attempts to communicate this desire to his/her environment. However, the message often received by those around him/her translates as "I need to control or set this individual straight. Consequently, I need to get on his/her back more than I have in the past." (p. 29)

In summary, choice theory focuses on knowledge of why and how the mind works; reality therapy focuses on strategies and techniques for dealing with human choices. Therefore, reality therapy is the delivery system. If choice theory is the train track, reality therapy is the train. If choice theory is the highway, reality therapy is the vehicle delivering the product (Wubbolding & Brickell, 2007). Wubbolding (1989, 2000a, 2008a) has formulated reality therapy as the WDEP system (wants, doing, evaluation, planning). In education, reality therapy, known as lead management, operationalizes, applies, and conveys choice theory principles to clients, students, parents, educators, employees, or other consumer of services. Even though educators do not provide therapy, they implement the principles of internal control psychology when they teach and use choice theory in their pedagogical endeavors. When educators understand how the mind works, according to choice theory, and how to communicate with the

WDEP system of reality therapy, learning increases and behavior improves (Wubbolding, 2000a). Reality therapy focuses on skills for dealing with people of any age, race, social status, culture, or gender who present with a wide variety of diagnoses (i.e., all behaviors or choices).

While the differences between theory and practice are clear, on the grassroots level the terms *choice theory* and *reality therapy* are often used imprecisely. Of necessity and quite appropriately, training sessions in reality therapy include explanation and discussion of the theoretical foundation as well as the delivery system reality therapy.

3

Choice Theory

HOW THE MIND WORKS: CHOICE THEORY

A theory of human behavior explains how people generate actions, cognition, and feelings and the resulting impact on physiology. It also presents information and elucidation about human motivation—that is, why people do what they do and how they make alternate choices. The following case provides a context for understanding a student's motivation and behavior.

CASE OF NOEL

Noel, a high school graduate, moves into the residence hall of a small college and enrolls as a freshman, soon to discover that he hates the school. The courses are too hard and the college rules too strict for him, and he misses his high school friends and family. Failing to study, he flunks most of his courses in the first semester. However, for some reason he decides to apply himself during the second semester and enter into the life of the college. At the end of the school year, his remarkable performance demonstrates a 180-degree turn. He finds the school enjoyable and is motivated to return for his sophomore year. How and why did his feelings change? What motivated him to decide to apply himself? Choice theory provides a complete explanation.

PSYCHOLOGICAL DEVELOPMENT

From its inception, choice theory has provided an explanation of mental health and a reconceptualization of mental and emotional disturbance. Behavior is seen as chosen; mental and emotional disturbance is described as unhappiness; even psychosis is a person's best effort to attain internal control. Human beings choose behaviors effective or ineffective for satisfying their inner drives or a combination of both. Figure 3.1 describes mental health as developmental—as a series of effective choices. It also describes mental disturbance as regressive or a series of ineffective choices.

Central to choice theory are human needs as motivators described as genetic instructions. Glasser (2003) states, "Choice theory explains that we are born with purpose built into our genes. Essentially our genes provide us with five basic needs that motivate all our behavior from birth to death" (p. 94). Mental health is seen as an accumulation of behaviors: effective or ineffective (Glasser, 1984), responsible or irresponsible (Glasser, 1972), positive or negative (Wubbolding, 2008a, 2008b, 2009a).

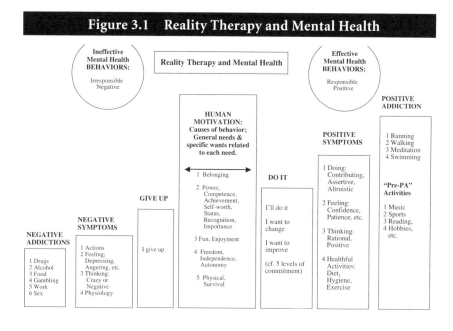

Figure 3.1   Reality Therapy and Mental Health

From *Using Reality Therapy* (p. 127), by R. Wubbolding, 1988, New York, NY: Harper & Row. Copyright 1988 by Robert E. Wubbolding. Adapted with permission.

Effective mental health is developmental, and ineffective mental health is regressive. The developmental pathway—as well as its opposite, the regressive pathway—represent two general processes that include specific choices influenced by genetics, family, environment, and culture. Two practical implications of this conceptualization of mental health are the importance of early intervention and the varying applications to individuals from a wide range of cultures.

MENTAL HEALTH AS AN ALTERNATIVE TO MENTAL DISORDERS

Choice theory and reality therapy constitute an alternative to the current and necessary attention placed on mental disorders. From the perspective of choice theory as well as from a logical point of view, there is a negative one-to-one correlation between mental health and its absence, between effective living and mental disorders. Consequently choice theory and reality therapy should be seen as a mental health system rather than a mere remedial system. The components of mental health have been the subject of study by mental health professionals for decades. Moore (1944) spoke of mental hygiene as a "practical science, which studies the human personality and its deviations (mental disorders) from ideal perfection with a view to their prevention" (p. 2). He added that control of emotions and drives formed a balanced personality. Kratochwill and Morris (1993) described the mental hygiene movement as a significant force in the development of interest in child and adolescent mental health. Similarly, Cavanagh and McGoldrick (1953) presented mentally healthy individuals as having a future orientation, satisfaction with daily activities, acceptance of society's standards, a willingness to correct mistakes, adaptation to life changes, and an emotional life steady and stable. Additionally, Freud frequently spoke of *leben und arbeiten* (love and work) as signaling mental health.

Maslow (Patterson, 1974), widely known for his hierarchy of needs, extended the concept of mental health by researching characteristics of self-actualizing people. Among the 14 qualities are openness to experience, acceptance of self and others, autonomy or independence of culture and environment, deep feeling of empathy for other human beings, healthy interpersonal relationships, and a non-hostile sense of humor. Wubbolding (2006) describes how the qualities of self-actualizing people can serve as goals satisfying the five needs described in choice theory. Moreover, part of the practice of reality therapy is to teach clients the principles of internal control psychology (Glasser, 2007). Consequently, with appropriate timing, clients can be taught the five-fold motivational system of human needs and be helped to incorporate the qualities as desirable goals and thus replace current misery. They learn that their behavior originates from within and is not thrust upon them by the external world or by their own personal experiences.

Effective or Growth Behaviors

A pattern of positive choices, or effective behaviors, characterizes a healthy and productive lifestyle, the opposite of regressive behaviors leading to less effective mental health and even mental disorders. These effective developmental behaviors constitute valuable ways to fulfill the human needs and motivational drives: survival or self-preservation, belonging, power or inner control, freedom or independence, fun or enjoyment. When chosen, these behaviors serve to replace the negative stages and can be incorporated into the therapeutic process as pathways to happiness and productive living. The stages of growth or effective behavior are as follows:

Stage 1: "I'll do it." "I want to improve." "I am committed to change."

Clients make explicit or implicit statements by which they demonstrate a willingness to make more effective choices. This stage, like its negative mirror image, is only transitory. As seen in Figure 3.1 clients often verbalize their level of commitment, or how much energy they will exert in taking more effective control of their lives. These statements do not exist in isolation. Rather, they accompany the positive symptomatology seen in stage 2.

Stage 2: Positive Symptoms

From the perspective of reality therapy, behavior is a global term that includes action, thinking or cognition, emotions or feelings, and physiology. This inclusive definition of behavior illustrates that thinking and feelings are not static conditions but are vibrant energies that are purposeful and inextricably connected with action. Signs of healthy conduct (actions), emotionality, and cognition include effective need-satisfying choices leading to less frustration and increased happiness. This is not to imply that healthy individuals never exhibit the negative symptoms described above. Even the most fulfilled people can occasionally choose actions that are less than efficacious. They can feel feelings and think thoughts that block their path to contentedness and impede their performance. Nevertheless, the following total behaviors describe internally generated symptoms or signs of effective need fulfillment and more fruitful and constructive living:

- *Actions.* Effective choices aimed at satisfying human needs embrace both assertive and altruistic behaviors. Healthy people clarify what they want, choose accordingly, and contribute to society through family, employment, civic life, and personal pursuits. Clearly, the action component of total behavior is the focus of the therapeutic process because of its accessibility to change.
- *Thinking.* Rational thinking is the mirror image of cognitive disturbance. Wubbolding (2003) states,

> Among the many rational thinking patterns implicit in reality therapy are a realistic understanding of what one can and cannot control, acceptance of what is unchangeable, and knowledge that one is responsible for one's own behavior. Therefore, the perception that all early childhood traumas must of their nature continue to victimize a person's adulthood is rejected. (p. 259)

Self-talk statements congruent with choice theory and the opposite of ineffective thinking are: (a) "I can, I am gaining more effective control of my life, and I am worthwhile"; (b) "I am happiest when I live within reasonable boundaries"; and (c) "I cannot control other people, but I can control my own behavior" (Wubbolding, 2009a). Glasser (2000a) emphasizes that clients incorporate the principles of choice theory into their thinking. In dealing with Lucy, a difficult client, he states, "It'll take some time but I will teach her that all any of us can control is our own *present* behavior" (p. 32).

- *Feelings.* The result of changes in action and thinking is change in human emotions. Increased patience, trust, self-confidence, magnanimity, mercy, empathy, sociability, acceptance, enthusiasm, and hope are among the emotions that flow from choices centering on action and thinking.
- *Physiology.* The final symptom of a constructive lifestyle is attending to one's physical needs. Persons living a full life and having a wide range of choices realize that need satisfaction is enhanced with proper diet, reasonable exercise, and health monitoring.

Thus, all human behavior, whether effective or ineffective, includes four components. Because human beings have the most direct control over their conduct or actions, they experience an immediate or, more often, an eventual change in feelings, cognition, and physiology when they make an action-focused change. The depressed person choosing to exercise, to reach out to others, or to do anything satisfying human needs has a high likelihood of achieving some relief.

Stage 3: Positive Addictions

The third stage of effective mental health, positive addiction, is unattained and unattainable for most people. Individuals can be quite healthy without a positive addiction. Positive addictions are activities that enhance mental health, satisfy human needs, and add a sense of inner control to a person's life (Glasser, 1976). Examples are running and meditation. These activities are performed noncompetitively, non-compulsively, and for a limited time on a regular basis. Becoming positively addicted requires a protracted amount of time, often 12 to 18 months. Such behaviors, as well as others that approach positive addiction (prepositive addiction "activities"), are the opposite of negative addictions. Rather than being self-destructive, positive addictions enhance psychological development and increase feelings of self-worth and accomplishment.

As with the negative stages, the positive stages signifying effective mental health do not exist as mutually exclusive groupings. Human beings can make effective choices at times and at other times choose ineffectively. Some psychotic persons can, at times, choose behaviors that most people would label as "sane." Similarly, even the healthiest person is capable of unhealthy or ineffective choices at times, such as occasional depression, chronic resentment, and bouts with guilt or shame.

Moreover, when interpreting human behavior through the lens of choice theory, the therapist considers a person's chronological age and psychological development. Thus in consulting with parents regarding their children, the reality therapist suggests that they spend time with the child during which both parent and child satisfy their needs for belonging and fun. This special time is adapted to the needs and wants of both parties. Finally, from the perspective of choice theory, the positive psychological development of individuals or regression to ineffective mental health results from a series of choices and accompanying feedback received from the world around us. These choices are complex and involve the interdependence and influence of family, community, and culture (Wubbolding & Brickell, 2001).

Ineffective or Regressive Behaviors

Mental disturbance or mental illness is not viewed as a static pathological condition. In choice theory the stages of regression are active behaviors generated for the purpose of satisfying the five internal genetic needs, with the result of achieving happiness. In the history of choice theory the regressive stages have been grouped as failure-directed or irresponsible (Glasser, 1972). But the most useful way to describe them is a person's best but quite ineffective effort to fulfill human needs (Glasser, 2005a, 2005b). More emphatically Glasser (1998) states,

> For all practical purposes, we choose *everything* we do, including the misery we feel. Other people can neither make us miserable nor make us happy. All we can get from them or give to them is information. But by itself information cannot make us do or feel anything. It goes into our brains, and then we decide what to do. . . . Choice theory teaches that we are much more in control of our lives than we realize. (pp. 3–4)

Consequently, a person's gradual deterioration of mental health is the result of behaviors generated from within and is best seen as having at least some element of control, an element of choice.

Stage 1: Giving Up

Behaviors characterizing this stage include listlessness, withdrawal, and apathy. Attempts to satisfy the five needs have been unsuccessful or frustrated because of ineffective choices or external circumstances. Wubbolding (2003) states, "The only alternative that appears reasonable is to cease trying. This stage is quite temporary and is followed by the symptoms of the more identifiable second stage" (p. 258).

Stage 2: Negative Symptoms

As people regress, they demonstrate ineffective mental health with negative symptoms. These behaviors represent their failed efforts to satisfy their internal motivations or genetic needs. However, these internally generated behaviors lead to added frustration, misery, unhappiness, and often conflict with the law, family, or societal expectations. Behaviors descriptive of these symptoms include:

- *Actions.* Negative or ineffective actions range from mildly acting out to compulsive, chaotic, and aggressive antisocial choices such as abuse, suicide, or homicide. Actions harmful to self or others, as well as their opposite—effective actions—are more clearly seen as chosen. Actions represent the component of behavior over which human beings have the most direct control and are more readily accepted as such by clients and professional therapists.

- *Thinking.* Cognition also is an attempt to fulfill needs. One need only to reflect on mental ruminations endlessly repeated during a sleepless night. These reiterated thoughts often focus on problem solving or dealing with daily frustrations. More disturbed cognition is also an attempt to satisfy needs. Such efforts sometimes seem to control others, but they can be self-defeating or even harmful to self and others. The word *disturbance* applies in a wide sense to pessimistic cognition ranging from the chronic negativism to severe psychotic delusions and hallucinations. Accompanying many ineffective actions are two categories of self-defeating thoughts—negative and crazy thoughts. Those described by Ellis & Harper (1997) include: (a) "I *must* do well and win the approval of others for my performances or else I am no good"; (b) "Other people *must* treat me considerately, fairly, kindly, and in exactly the way I want them to treat me"; and (c) "I *must* get what I want when I want it; and I *must* not get what I don't want." Spiegler (2008) describes the characteristics of these irrational self-verbalizations as absolutistic thinking, overgeneralizing, and catastrophizing. While these irrational statements can be congruent with choice theory, still there are many identifiable self-talk thoughts that spring more explicitly from choice theory (Wubbolding, 2000a): (a) "I can't, I am powerless, I am worthless"; (b) "No one is going to tell me what to do"; and (c) "I can control other people" (p. 68).

While rational emotive behavioral therapy (REBT) sees thinking as the cause of mental disturbance, choice theory posits cognition as accompanying actions and feelings, not as *causes* of actions or feelings. Rather, cognitions are thinking behaviors coinciding with action behaviors. For instance, a person feeling depressed often immobilizes himself or herself regarding actions and tells himself or herself, "Life is useless," "I'm powerless," and so on. This total behavior springs from unmet inner needs.

- *Feelings.* Wubbolding (2000a, 2009a) describes negative emotions as representing mild upsetness at one end of the spectrum of human feelings to acute and debilitating depression, anger, shame, guilt, resentment, vengeance, rage, and similar feelings from the "worried well" (Talmon, 1990) to phobic disorders.
- *Physiology.* Physical ailments are best treated with appropriate medical attention. However, some physical symptoms can be the result of consistently ineffective attempts aimed at satisfying needs. These behaviors sometimes are "in excess of what would be expected from the history, physical examination or laboratory findings. The symptoms are not intentionally produced or feigned" (*Diagnostic and Statistical Manual of Mental Disorders-IV-TR,* 2000, p. 490). Many physiological symptoms "are best treated not only with good medical care but also through counseling or psychotherapy designed to help the client make better choices that is, to choose positive symptoms" (Wubbolding, 2003, p. 258). Choice theory and the delivery system reality therapy embrace the ethical principles related to standard practice, such as making referrals when client issues are outside one's scope of practice.

The "Ethical Principles of Psychologists and Code of Conduct" (American Psychological Association, 2002) states, "Psychologists provide services, teach, and conduct research with populations and in areas only within the boundaries of their competence" (2.01) and "When indicated and professionally appropriate, psychologists cooperate with other professionals in order to serve their clients/patients effectively and appropriately" (3.09).

From the choice theory point of view, all behavior is composed of four components: action, thinking, feeling, and physiology. Therefore, it is referred to as "total behavior." The theory described here carries the label *choice theory* because of the emphasis on behavior as chosen. However, the framing of behavior as chosen does not mean that human beings have complete control over each component of behavior. Rather, actions are most under our control, followed by thinking, feelings, and finally physiology, over which we have the least direct control.

Stage 3: Negative Addictions

The final stage of regressive behavior or ineffective mental health is negative addictions. From the point of view of choice theory and reality therapy, negative addiction is biological/psychological, chronic, relapse inducing, social, occupational, familial, and often fatal. It affects all aspects of the addicted person's life. Consequently, many forms of intervention are needed. In implementing choice theory and reality therapy applied to addictions, the practitioner stresses choices over which clients have control: lifestyle, occupation, family, relationships, and, in general, productive living. Thus they can avoid controversial and debated issues about addictions, relapse, and recovery. The negative addictions to drugs, alcohol, and other substances as well as to activities such as gambling, work, sex, food, pornography, and the Internet represent the last regressive stage of ineffective behavioral attempts to fulfill needs.

These three stages of regressively ineffective behaviors should not be taken as rigidly discreet categories, exclusive of one another. Rather, they represent an exposition of gradual deterioration in human behavior related to need fulfillment. They are the mirror opposite of effective behaviors.

THE CASE OF NOEL REVISITED

Based on the explanation of psychological development described above, Noel did not find the college courses need-satisfying. Consequently, he gave up studying (stage 1) and lapsed into feelings of apathy, telling himself, "It's not worth the effort" (stage 2). Fortunately, he did not take the next step into drug abuse or addiction (stage 3). Finding failure even more unsatisfying than the effort required to pass his courses, he decided that success would satisfy his need for power and achievement as well as belonging. His first step was "I'll do it," followed immediately by action choices accompanied by "I can" self-talk. The result was the satisfaction of inner needs. All of this was brought about by realistically doable choices.

HUMAN MOTIVATION INNER CONTROL: COMPARISONS

The original term for the psychological explanation of human behavior is *control theory* or *control system theory*. Predecessors to the current adaptation to education and psychology included MacColl (1946), Wiener (1948, 1952), Pask (1976), and Sickles (1976). The most influential control theorist for Glasser was William Powers, alluded to in Chapter 2. Approximately the same age, they met several times to discuss how the cybernetic theory of brain functioning, control theory, could be adapted to psychotherapy and education and used by practitioners in a therapy office and in the classroom. In the foreword to Glasser's book, *Stations of the Mind* (1980), Powers states:

> Bill Glasser has invented an unusual method for learning a new theory: write a book about it. Judging from the result, I think I can recommend this method for those with the intellectual honesty, the energy, and the persistence to carry it through. (p. ix)

Glasser's contributions (1980, 1984, 1998) are explanations in plain language, his own additions and extensions, and applications to psychotherapy (2000a) and education (1990, 2000b, 2005a, 2005b). Most recently, he has added applications to human relationships (2007).

INTERNAL CONTROL

Choice theory holds several principles in common with other theories. As an internal control system, it holds as true the philosophical and psychological postulate that human behavior originates from within the human being. Contrary to popular belief, human beings cannot "make" other people do what they want them to do. Force and threats directed to others can be effective only when the coerced person wants to conform—that is, to satisfy the needs described below. Of course, the possibility of severe punishment or harsh consequences can be quite persuasive for many people but do not automatically result in conformity. Many people choose to die a martyr's death rather than reject their deeply held values or beliefs.

Other theories of psychotherapy also embrace the idea of internal control as a foundational principle. Mosak and Maniacci (2008) state,

> According to the Adlerian conception, people are not pushed by causes; that is, they are not determined by heredity and environment. . . . People move toward self-selected goals that they feel will give them a place in the world, will provide them with security, and will preserve their self-esteem. (p. 64)

In describing internal motivation as seen from the Adlerian perspective, Slavik, Sperry, and Carlson (2000) describe one internal motivator: overcoming life's challenges. They state, "Behavior is then directed by this image of the goal. Motivation 'pulls' the individual: behavior is then motivated by the final goal and the individual's concern for the future" (p. 250).

Similarly, Albert Ellis, the founder of rational emotive behavior therapy (REBT), has consistently maintained that most psychological problems and disturbances are not caused by external forces but by self-defeating cognition:

> No matter how defective people's heredity may be, and no matter what trauma they have experienced, the *main* reason why they now usually overreact or under react to adversities is that they now have some dogmatic, irrational, unexamined beliefs. They are often deifications and devilifications of themselves and others, and they tend to

wane when empirically checked, logically disputed and shown to be impractical. (Ellis, 2008, p. 189)

Ellis was fond of quoting Epictetus, "Men are disturbed not by things but by the views they take of them." A related theory, cognitive therapy, founded by Aaron Beck, posits cognition as the root of mental disturbance. For example, depression is rooted in a negative view of self, the world, or the future. A depressed person feels worthless, abandoned, and insufficient to cope with his or her circumstances. This hopeless worldview stems from biases in processing information. Cognitive therapists assist clients to alter their thinking and to take action aimed at dealing with inertia and fatigue. As Beck and Weishaar (2008) state, "Refuting negative expectations and demonstrating motor ability play important roles in recovery" (p. 273).

According to the existential therapy, the bedrock value is

the uncanny core to be found at the heart of existence and the spirit of inquiry that resides at the deepest level of consciousness. This spirit of inquiry is found, by extension, in all approaches to psychotherapy worthy of the name. (Mendelowitz & Schneider, 2008, p. 303)

They add that existential therapists such as Rollo May give primacy to freedom and destiny. Human beings are free to choose their destiny in a social and cultural context within limits. "The polarities of freedom and destiny, no less than the challenges implied, are essential to existential conceptions of psychological health" (Mendelowitz & Schneider, 2008, p. 306). In summarizing existential theory, Corey (2009) states that existentialism does not include any special style of practicing psychotherapy. Rather, it represents a way of thinking and is not a separate school or model with unique techniques. He states, "The existential approach rejects the deterministic view of human nature" (p. 133). He then elaborates on the internal control of existentialism: "Existential therapists . . . emphasize our freedom to choose what to make of our circumstances. We are not victims of circumstance because, to a large extent, we are what we choose to be" (p. 133).

The theme of internal control as a basic principle of psychotherapeutic theories continues in gestalt therapy. Yontef and Jacobs (2008) describe *organismic self-regulation*: Human beings learn to identify with what they believe, sense, feel, observe, and want. They grow when they become aware of how others impact them and how they impact others:

> One moves toward wholeness by identifying with ongoing experience, being in contact with what is actually happening, identifying and trusting what one genuinely feels and wants and being honest with self and others about what one is actually willing and able to do—or not willing to do. (p. 329)

Gestalt therapy recognizes conscious awareness and the internal origin of human behavior as integral to both theory and practice. Frew (2008) further emphasizes the importance of the continuous relationship between the person and the environment and that human beings, starting with their own behavior, have the power to impact the world around them.

Multimodal therapy, an eclectic system based on social learning theory, communications theory, and many other sources, encompasses the total internal experience of the human being such as cognition, imagination, emotions, senses, and human relationships. Lazarus (2008) has formulated the BASIC I.D., and states, "Human life and conduct are products of ongoing *b*ehaviors, *a*ffective processes, *s*ensations, *i*mages, *c*ognitions, *i*nterpersonal relationships and *b*iological functions" (p. 369). In describing the techniques used in multimodal therapy, Sharf (2008) states that multimodal therapy draws on a larger pool than most therapies. Clearly these techniques, such as free association, image exploration, and the Adlerian technique of "acting as if," assume an internal control psychology, one that emphasizes the ability of clients to change their behavior and the circumstances of their lives.

In summary, choice theory shares several underlying principles with other counseling theories, including the inner origin of human behavior, the power of the person to make changes in his or her life, the curative properties of healthy interpersonal relationships, the use of a wide number of techniques for implementing theory, and the implied hopefulness for a better personal future. Choice theory adds many dimensions to counseling and psychotherapy, especially the explicit emphasis and exquisite nature of human choice.

HUMAN MOTIVATION–HUMAN NEEDS: WHY PEOPLE DO WHAT THEY DO

Choice theory provides a comprehensive explanation of human behavior. Its purview ranges from effective behaviors often described as mentally healthy, in-control, and self-actualizing to minimally and severely ineffective or out-of-control behaviors, such as those described in the *DSM-IV-TR*. Contrary to current criticism (Sue & Sue, 1999) that counseling and psychotherapy theories founded in a Euro-American context are culture bound, choice theory addresses behaviors of individuals and groups representing cultures from every continent. The delivery system reality therapy, summarized in the acronym WDEP, applies to individuals and groups from virtually every ethnicity (Mickel, 2005; Wubbolding, 1989, 1991, 2000a; Wubbolding, Brickell, Imhof, Kim, Lojk, & Al-Rashidi, 2004). In speaking of reality therapy as used in Korea, Kim and Hwang (2006) state,

> Since 1986 reality therapy and choice theory have been introduced to the counseling and business fields in Korea followed with much research . . . it is embraced by professionals, including counselors, educators, psychologists, psychiatrists, social workers and others, as well as parents. (p. 25)

Citing several research studies in the Malaysian language, Jazimin Jusoh, Mahmud, and Mohd Ishak (2008) state, "These works are testimony that reality therapy, when applied in suitable modules, can be beneficial for clients of various backgrounds" (p. 5).

Because of the emphasis on human behavior as chosen and due to major expansions in control theory, Glasser renamed the foundational principles and the developments of control theory *choice theory*. It remains an internal control system in that behavior is not thrust on human beings from the external environment or culture nor determined by past experiences or parental persuasion. Though these influences can leave their imprint, they do not nullify free choice.

Choice theory is based on the principle that human motivation is a "here and now" phenomenon. As a psychological explanation, choice theory posits five human needs from which springs choice (Glasser, 1998,

2005a, 2008). These needs are seen as genetic and therefore universal. They are not culture bound, not limited to any racial or ethnic group. Rather, they are motivators that drive the behavior of all human beings.

Survival or Self-Preservation

The psychological needs described below are housed in the cerebral cortex, sometimes referred to as the "new brain" because of its more recent development in the history of human kind. It sometimes receives a help-me signal from the autonomic nervous system that houses the "old brain," the place of the survival or self-preservation need. It causes the system to resist disease, to feel hunger and thirst, to seek physical homeostasis, and to pursue sexual gratification. Characteristic of all biological sensate creatures, the need for self-preservation drives the organism to maintain life. And yet, human living is more complicated than mere self-preservation. The satisfaction of survival often occurs not in isolation but as a motivation interdependent with the satisfaction of other needs. Twenty-first century survival requires at least some human interaction, successful endeavors, and effective choices. Enjoying life also provides need satisfaction and is often an additional benefit. Glasser (1998) states, "It is these additional lifelong needs beyond survival that make our lives so complicated, so different from those of animals" (p. 33).

Belonging, Love, Affiliation

Human beings possess an innate need for human closeness and for interdependence. While the genetic origin of this need remains hypothetical, belonging and other needs provide a basis and a pathway for effective therapy. Two examples illustrating the efficacy of satisfying the need for belonging in a constructive manner can be found in stories of forced confinement and captivity.

Nien Cheng's Interrogations

Cheng (1986) tells the story of her 6-year solitary confinement during the Maoist regime in China and how she coped with her almost overwhelming loneliness and isolation and the accompanying passivity and depression. Within the rigid restrictions imposed upon her, she gained a sense of belonging by shouting her answers during her interrogations. She satisfied her need for belonging as best she could, believing that other prisoners in the same building could hear her voice. Thus, her shouting was her way of gaining a sense belonging with them as well as communicating a source of courage to them. She also tells of an increased sense of power accompanying this deep feeling of belonging.

Fred and Porter's Bond

Hirsch (2004) presents a story of heroic courage and human bonding. Fred Cherry and Porter Halyburton, fighter pilots and prisoners of war in Vietnam, suffered unspeakable psychological and physical tortures during their nearly seven years internment. Major Fred Cherry, an African American Air Force pilot, was raised in a segregated world. Shot down and wounded, he suffered additional torture at the hands of his captors, adding to his pain and suffering. U.S. Navy Lieutenant Junior Grade Porter Halyburton, a White man raised in the South in the 1940s and '50s, became Fred's cellmate. Their legendary closeness saved both of them. Porter nursed Fred, who received extremely primitive treatment for his injuries, including several operations and poor postoperative treatment. He helped Fred by bathing and exercising him, while Fred supported him psychologically for 7 months. Fred taught Porter the lessons of heroism, loyalty, and a bias-free worldview. Because of their synergistic union, they both survived and carried with them during the rest of their imprisonment the desire to survive, not only to rejoin their families, but to see each other again and resume their friendship. Another prisoner, Giles Norrington, a Navy pilot shot down in 1968, recalled,

> By the time I arrived, Porter and Fred had already achieved legendary status . . . the respect, mutual support, and affection that had developed between them were the stuff of sagas. Their stories as individuals and as a team, were a great source of inspiration. (Hirsch, 2004, pp. 9–10)

As Hirsch noted,

> Many of the POWs had to cross racial, cultural, or social boundaries to exist in such close confines. But Halyburton and Cherry did more than coexist—they rescued each other. Each man credits the other

with saving his life. One needed to be saved physically; the other, emotionally. In doing so, they forged a brotherhood that no enemy could shatter. (p. 10)

In November 2004 Fred and Porter appeared on C-SPAN. They once again stated that they would do the same again for each other. Parenthetically, Fred stated that he has never once dreamed about Vietnam, illustrating a principle crucial to reality therapy: Human relationships alleviate pain and can even lessen post-traumatic stress.

These anecdotes illustrate the life-sustaining nature of the human effort to satisfy the need for belonging. On the operational level, reality therapists see belonging as the most prominent need. Regardless of the presenting issue, the effective use of reality therapy includes a therapeutic alliance as a foundation for assisting clients to improve their interpersonal relationships. Wubbolding (2005) states, "Enhanced acquaintanceships, friendships and intimacies provide the royal road to mental health and quality living" (p. 44).

Inner Control, Power, Achievement, Self-Esteem, Recognition

Originally referred to as power, the third human motivator or source of behavior covers a variety of concepts. Satisfying the need for power does not equate with dominating or controlling other human beings. Fulfilling this need is not a zero sum game. There need not be winners and losers in the quest for power. Rather, individuals choose activities aimed at helping them gain a sense of inner control, the perception that they are in charge of their lives, that they have achieved or accomplished something. For instance, upon being released from the hospital after a successful surgical procedure, the patient experiences a sense of inner control, a feeling of being in charge of her own life.

Even competitors often feel an intense sense of accomplishment not merely because they have triumphed over others but because they have demonstrated to themselves and others their highest level of achievement. At the 2008 Olympics in Beijing, Carol Huynh won the first Canadian gold medal in wrestling. Hawthorn (2008) described how the Huynh family arrived in Canada after fleeing from Vietnam in 1978. Carol's parents watched her from the stands weeping and cheering. Neither they nor Carol herself described this accomplishment as defeating an opponent. Rather they spoke of the discipline required as well as the support she received from her coach, her family, and the people from Hazelton, British Columbia, and from her current home in Calgary, Alberta. Her coach, Debbie Brauer, stated, "Kinship is very strong. It's a community that, despite its problems, really does pull together. It's not what you do for a living, or what color your skin is, but who you are that matters" (p. 7).

On the other hand, the urge to triumph in competition also satisfies the power need. The desire to win an election, to defeat the opponent, to triumph over the other team creates the feeling of power and achievement. Some people choose to satisfy their need for power by conquering and exploiting others emotionally, intellectually, and even physically. Fulfilling this need with little concern for the needs of others explains antisocial and even Axis-II behaviors, often providing a substitute for a person's inability to satisfy belonging in an appropriate manner.

Human beings desire the self-perception of being capable of achieving, of accomplishing something, of pride, status, and importance. For the most part, they seek these inner satisfactions in a positive, effective, or mentally healthy manner. But they sometimes attempt to fulfill these needs in ways that are self-destructive or harmful to others. In discussing choice theory applied to juvenile delinquents and their need for recognition, Myers and Jackson (2002) state,

> The juveniles have been lectured by the best. What they have not gotten is praise for doing a good job. They have not received approval from those they love and respect. They have not been rewarded for a job well done. And, the touch they have received may have been the back of someone's hand. Let juveniles know when they do well. (p. 199)

Many people attempt need satisfaction, especially fulfilling their need for status or importance, by the abuse of drugs, which consequently creates the illusion of need satisfaction. They gain the momentary perception of being in charge of their own lives, but they have deluded themselves. When the illusion fades, the feeling of power or achievement disintegrates, often resulting in a deepening sense of powerlessness.

Freedom, Independence, Autonomy

The fourth human motivator urges people to search for options, to select among possibilities, and to make specific choices. Depending on culture and experience, human beings seek independence or autonomy in varying degrees and in diverse ways, either life enhancing or damaging to self or others. Uncovering satisfactory options constitutes a primary goal in the practice of reality therapy. As with other needs, the external world imposes natural or environmental limits on human choice. Still, the practitioner of reality therapy avoids falling into the trap of agreeing with the oft-stated refrain, "I have no choice." As Glasser (1998) states, "There is always a choice."

Viktor Frankl (1984) based his logotherapy on the principle that no matter how dire the circumstances, the human person has a choice. During his 3 years of imprisonment at Auschwitz, he believed he had a choice, not regarding actions but how he would *perceive* the diabolical world of the concentration camp. Carl Rogers frequently described a hypothetical prisoner in solitary confinement tapping on the wall in Morse code, "Is anybody out there?" After years of engaging in the only choice available, he hears a response: "Yes, I am on the other side of the wall." The prisoner must have experienced an intense feeling of liberation and even exhilaration.

People express and fulfill the need for freedom in a variety of ways. Some people have a high need for freedom and seem to tolerate little restriction or structure. Others feel free when they are required to conform to a predictable routine. When asking participants in training sessions "What do you like about your job?" many respond that they know what to expect on their jobs. Others state, "No two days are alike." Clearly some individuals enjoy a maximum amount of variety, while others find need satisfaction in a more organized work environment.

Fun, Enjoyment

Aristotle defined a human as a creature that is risible—that is, it can laugh. Choice theory embraces the principle that people have an innate need or motivation that directs but does not compel their behavior toward fun or at least enjoyment. From the cradle to the grave, human beings find ways to be comfortable and to enjoy their surroundings. Moreover, Glasser (1998) connects the need for fun with learning:

> We are the only land-based creatures who play all our lives and because we learn all our lives, the day we stop playing is the day we stop learning. People who fall in love are learning a lot about each other and they find themselves laughing almost continually. One of the first times infants laugh is when someone plays peek-a-boo with them. I believe they laugh because that game teaches them something very useful. They learn, I am I and you are you. (p. 41)

Wubbolding (2000a) states, "The developmental task of differentiating oneself from others involves the deep inner need for fun" (p. 16). Other developmental tasks are facilitated by enjoyment. Adolescents and adults, young and old, seek personal adjustment by redirecting their thoughts and actions from life's problems to pleasant endeavors. A major task for a therapist implementing choice theory is helping clients make positive and often delectable choices leading to a sense of inner joy.

When counseling couples and families, the effective reality therapist assists them in planning to have fun together, suggests Wubbolding (2000a, 2000b). He also states, "If they have achieved a high degree of intimacy, they have spent time together learning. A therapist, using reality therapy, helps clients have fun together, do enjoyable activities as a (unit), laugh at themselves and at the foibles of others. The comedian Victor Borge has said that the shortest distance between two people is a laugh" (Wubbolding, 2000a, p. 16).

At first glance the role of fun in mental health might seem shallow and superficial. In discussing the role of enjoyment in a client's life with a therapist, it might appear that the therapist is facilitating an avoidance of deeper issues. The opposite, however, is true: A discussion of positive mental health provides an alternative to major and minor disorders. For example, diagnostic criteria for dysthymic disorders include low energy or fatigue and feelings of hopelessness. In terms of choice theory needs, these individuals do not effectively satisfy their need for fun.

Questioning clients about their need for fun is a useful starting point in the process of therapy with many clients. With oppositional adolescents, the reality therapist frequently asks them to "describe the last time you did something that was fun without getting in trouble or did something that would not have gotten you in trouble if your parents, teachers or police observed you doing it." This approach coincides with the Ericksonian axiom, "There is not a one-to-one correlation between the problem and the solution." To discuss fun with clients exemplifies reality therapy as a mental health system, not merely a system for reme-diating mental disorders. Sometimes the solution seems to have little to do with the problem.

Is There a Human Need for Spirituality, Faith, Meaning, or Purpose?

Staub and Pearlman (2002) describe a need for spirituality—that is, tran-scendence of the self. They state that in later life this need becomes more significant,

> but the groundwork for its satisfaction is laid all through life. We can fulfill it through spiritual experiences or connection to God or other spiritual entities . . . we can fulfill it by creating higher, more universal meaning in our lives. (p. 1)

In reviewing the literature on human needs, Litwack (2007) states,

> If one studies the history of mankind, it is difficult to dismiss the power of spirituality. Whether called a formal religion, humanism or a belief in nature, throughout history mankind seems to have had the need to believe in something other (higher, different) than oneself. (p. 30)

Frankl's logotherapy (1984) shares the emphasis on human decision and choice as a theoretical cornerstone. He also emphasizes meaning and pur-pose as a foundational principle for therapy and even for daily living. Frankl attributes his own sense of purpose, meaning, and faith as reasons for his surviving Auschwitz. He further associates the need for purpose and mean-ing with prisoners' survival more than their athletic and physical strength.

The use of reality therapy has been applied to spirituality in helping clients deepen their faith in the divine, to live a life spiritually oriented, and to focus on issues outside and larger than themselves (Carleton, 1994; Linnenberg, 1997; Tabata, 1999; Wubbolding, 1992). Many clients perceive that their problems and issues have a spiritual and moral dimension (Mickel & Liddie-Hamilton, 1996). In discussing family therapy, Mickel and Hall (2006) describe love as expressed in family life as holistic and spiritual. They assert that love is beyond the physical and mental world in that it lasts forever.

Choice theory as articulated by William Glasser places faith and spirituality as behaviors chosen to satisfy needs. On the other hand, he allows for faith as a need but not one of *his* formulations. He emphasizes that anyone instructing others about choice theory is free to add needs to the basic five, but it should be emphasized that the additional needs are beyond the original theory (Glasser, 2008).

CHARACTERISTICS OF NEEDS

The need system of choice theory serves as an inner motivational system. Human beings are driven to generate behaviors and make choices based on inner sources. They are not coerced, nor is their behavior determined by childhood experiences, culture, environment, or external rewards. Needs serve as engines producing actions, cognition, emotion, and even physiology, and they share several characteristics in common.

1. *General:* The needs are general not specific. For example, people have a need for belonging, not a need for a specific person. They have a need for fun but not for golf.
2. *Universal:* Human needs can be predicated of all human beings. This sweeping statement, while not empirically verified and perhaps not verifiable, designates the choice theory motivational system as multicultural, a unifying force for people of all racial and ethnic groups.
3. *Neutral:* While some individuals attempt to satisfy their needs by hurting or exploiting others, the components of the motivational system merely drive the behavior toward satisfaction rather than toward appropriateness or inappropriateness.

4. *Varying in level of intensity/strength:* Some people have a high need for belonging and often seek to satisfy it in productive ways, while others attempt to fulfill it by ingratiating themselves so as to exploit others. Some have a high need for freedom, while others require more structure and routine.

5. *Balanced:* Effective mental health includes some balance among the needs. Even if one need predominates, a well-functioning person does not completely neglect other needs. A hermit needs people . . . to stay away from!

6. *Mutually conflictual:* Satisfying the needs often means that a behavior fulfills more than one need. Friends have fun together. Needs can also be in conflict. For example, the motivation to satisfy freedom can interfere with the motivation to satisfy belonging.

7. *Interpersonally conflictual:* As is evident to any family therapist, parents and children engage in arguing, blaming, criticizing, and a host of other toxic behaviors. These behaviors originate when one person's need prevents another person from satisfying his or her need.

8. *Fulfilled moment to moment:* Individuals seek to survive, to be in control of their lives, and to fulfill other needs either consciously or unconsciously on a continuous basis. Consequently, behaviors are habitually generated to satisfy interpersonal relationships, make choices, or find enjoyment/fun.

9. *Overlapping:* The needs do not exist in isolated compartments. Rather, satisfying one need often satisfies another need. A golfer satisfies both power and fun when making a hole in one. Telling about the event adds to the need satisfaction by fulfilling belonging and adding to the range of need satisfaction.

10. *Undeniable:* The needs are the unrelenting and ultimate source of motivation. They are the foundational principle behind human behavior.

11. *Current:* Effective living results from motivation that is present and not imposed by past experience.

12. *Somewhat hierarchical:* Survival or self-preservation precedes the satisfaction of psychological needs. However, some individuals seek to gain power by destroying their own lives through suicide. Also,

satisfying the need for belonging can compensate for deficits in the ability to satisfy other needs. Emphasizing the prominence of the need for belonging, Glasser (2003, 2005a) teaches that dysfunctional interpersonal relationships are the root causes of many mental health problems.

In summary, the human need system is the ultimate source of behavior and occupies the center of choice theory. Reality therapy applications include an assessment of how clients satisfy and hope to satisfy their five needs. The rationale behind this process is that human choices are generated for a purpose: satisfying current internal desires related to five general needs. The process of therapy consists in helping clients examine their behavior, determine its effectiveness, and plan more effectively for the future.

SPECIFIC MOTIVATORS: WANTS OR QUALITY WORLD AND SCALES

Beginning at infancy, we interact with the world around us and discover experiences as pleasant or unpleasant. When these specific interactions with our environment are experienced as pleasant or need-satisfying, they become what Glasser has labeled the *quality world* or *world of wants*. Quality, in this context, means highly desirable and having personal value. All human beings, regardless of cultural influences, develop pictures or wants. These specific wants, circumscribed by family and cultural influences, are pictures of what is desirable, what is satisfying, what fulfills our needs. Infants quickly learn that crying gains them the attention needed for their physical and psychological comfort. They then realize that smiles and laughter help them develop satisfying relationships with family, neighbors, and other admirers. As children grow and interact with parents and teachers and have satisfying experiences, they insert the expectations of authority figures into their quality worlds as desirable. Conversely, if their experiences are unpleasant or distressful—that is, not need-satisfying—they are less likely to put education and related experiences into their quality world, their world of wants. Clearly, the content of the quality world and of specific wants varies significantly between cultures. People born in

Harare, Zimbabwe; Seoul, Korea; and the Loire valley of France have their respective quality worlds with quite different wants or pictures.

Wants or Quality World

Quality world wants include people, places, ideas, treasured possessions, and valued beliefs. From birth to death, the quality world constitutes a developing process. Each stage of human development embraces a changing story line. Adolescents' quality worlds—that is, specific wants satisfying their five needs—are quite different from those of middle-aged adults or senior citizens.

This inner world is called *quality* because human beings predicate quality, value, and importance to its content. Glasser (2003) describes the function of the quality world:

> Our quality world sets the standard for our life. It is a small, simulated world that we start to create in our memory shortly after birth. By the time we are two years old it is filled with need satisfying information, mostly in the form of pictures that we keep adjusting and updating all our lives. (p. 145)

The collection of wants and desires is analogous to a mental picture album that shows us, moment to moment, what we need and what we are attempting to match through input received from our senses (Glasser, 1984, 1998).

Specificity is the foundation of the quality world. Needs are general; wants are specific and unique to each individual. Wubbolding (2000a) states:

> Ideas about specific ways to gain power range from maintaining a reasonable weight to maintaining a high political office or reigning over a financial empire. Donald Trump's idea of a satisfying life is vastly different from the late Mother Theresa's picture. Specific pictures of freedom are also unique to each person. Satisfying to some persons is the structure of a 9–5 job with clear guidelines and routine responsibilities. Such people often feel free of the ambiguities and uncertainties that a lone entrepreneur feels. On the other hand,

a daily schedule can be very restrictive for people who view freedom differently. Similarly, perceptions of fun vary from person to person. One person sees sky diving as fun. Another, terrified by watching it on television, finds a casual walk to be exciting enough or even the epitome of enjoyment. Still another likes to play professional football while his opposite thinks exercise means filling the bath tub, sitting for a half hour, pulling the plug and fighting the current as the water rushes out. (p. 18)

The pictures contained in the quality world are specific, changeable, and developmental. Other characteristics include both the realistic and unrealistic attainability of wants. Human beings often seek an unattainable goal. An adolescent wants to "be left alone." A parent wants to control his or her adolescent. A nursing home resident insists, "I want to go home," even though failing health makes it impossible. The work of the therapist is to assist clients to formulate realistically achievable wants. Wants may also be vague or blurred. Skilled reality therapists assist clients to clearly define what they want from the world around them.

Another task of the therapist is helping clients set priorities among their wants, especially with clients having difficulty ranking their wants as important, less important, or even trivial, satisfying for the moment or on a more permanent basis. As Wubbolding (2000a) states, "A major developmental task for recovery from addictions, for both the addict and the family members, is to recognize that the fulfillment of some wants is more appropriately delayed" (p. 19). Reality therapists help recovering clients evaluate the effectiveness of their self-talk, "I want what I want when I want it and I want it now." They are well served if they gradually come to the realization that some wants are unrealistic, others unreasonable, and others helpful to recovery and to interpersonal relationships.

Even when the pictures or wants are specific, they may be blurred. A major part of the therapeutic process consists in helping clients clarify their imprecise goals, objectives, and hopes—that is, their *wants*. The oppositional adolescent wanting to be independent and "left alone" is often at a loss to describe more specifically the nature of being left alone. The therapist asks for a detailed clarification, helping the client describe exactly,

"What will it look like if you are left alone?" "What would you be doing in the next few days if you were to be free of any supervision?" "If someone were to observe you for 3 hours doing 'left alone' behaviors, what would they see?" The obsessive-compulsive client is treated in a similar way. Such a client wants to be free of the painful repetitious actions or thoughts but has not yet clarified a positive want that effectively drives his or her choices. Ridding one's self of pain or suffering does not constitute prolonged or effective motivation. Consequently the therapist assists the client to formulate a more positive picture of a desired behavior by astute questioning: "If you could set aside the distracting thoughts and repetitious actions, what would you do differently this afternoon or this evening?" "What pleasant thoughts would go through your mind if you were to abandon your painful thinking?" A depressed person often feels overwhelmed by darkness and hopelessness. The therapist helps to reframe these feelings from debilitating emotions to clear and efficacious wants: "Do you want to feel joyful and more upbeat?" "What would you be doing if you were to be feeling even slightly better?" A family therapist assists the family members to clarify their common, individual, and even contradictory wants. If the family exerts sufficient effort in unblurring their wants and looking for commonality in them, they are more likely to reconcile differences and to function as a more well-adjusted family. The therapists' responsibility in this familial effort is multiplied exponentially.

The quality world, containing specific wants related to more generic needs, serves as the second source of motivation. It constitutes the world we would like to live in, one that often requires clarification, self-evaluation, prioritization, and discussion with a trusted friend, colleague, family member, or therapist.

Scales

The quality world constitutes the collection of specific desires and wants related to needs. When a person perceives that he or she is fulfilling a want, it is as though a mental scale is in balance. On the other hand, when human beings do not satisfy their mental pictures, there is a gap between what is desired and what is achieved. Analogous to an out-of-balance scale and depending on the intensity of the want, human beings experience a sense of frustration ranging from a minor or trifling degree to an intense or severe degree. For example, an infant wants comfort and experiences discomfort. This out-of-balance scale is experienced as a frustration or more accurately, it results in a frustration signal. A parent wanting a child to achieve in school and perceiving the child failing experiences a severe out-of-balance scale. A person rejected by a lover often sustains a long-lasting out-of-balance scale. The person wants the relationship, does not have the relationship, and is unable to regain the relationship. The result: ongoing frustration, a sense of powerlessness, and an unfulfilled need for belonging.

The out-of-balance scale is neither good nor bad, appropriate nor inappropriate, congruous nor incongruous. It does, however, send a signal—more accurately, a frustration signal—represented by the jagged arrow in Figure 3.2 activating the behavioral system. It is the trigger for problem solving and for purposeful behavior aimed at the external world. On the operational level, reality therapists treat behaviors, especially actions, as choices.

Due to the emphasis on behavior as chosen, the theory underlying the practice of reality therapy is called choice theory (Glasser, 1998). One of the basic goals of reality therapy is to help clients make more effective choices. Treating behavior as a choice does not equate with complete control of every component of the behavioral system. On a practical level, the "as if" principle applies. Behavior is treated as a choice even if clients are reluctant to admit they have any power over their behavior. Part of the practice of reality therapy consists in helping clients realize that they have more control, even if not complete control, over their behavior than previously thought.

TOTAL BEHAVIORAL SYSTEM

Seen from the perspective of choice theory, as discussed earlier, total behavior includes four components: action, thinking or cognition, feelings or emotions, and physiology. The suitcase of behavior in Figure 3.2 illustrates another characteristic: the inseparability of the four components of total behavior. Behavior is analogous to a suitcase with four levels or modules. The handle, attached to the action level of the suitcase, illustrates the

Figure 3.2   Choice Theory: Motivational System

Human behavior originates from five human needs. As human beings develop, they formulate specific wants unique to each person. These are stored in the perceived world along with memories. Perceiving the discrepancy (out-of-balance scale) between what one has and what one wants, human beings choose behavior that is purposeful and directed toward the world around them. The goal is to gain perceptions. These perceptions are filtered through three lenses or perceptual filters.

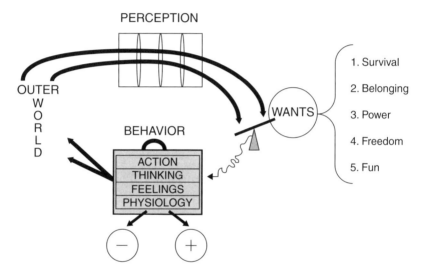

From *How the Brain Works*, by W. Glasser, 2005, Chatsworth, CA: The William Glasser Institute. Copyright 2005 by The William Glasser Institute. Adapted with permission.

more explicit nature of choice. Human beings can control actions more effectively than other components of the behavioral system and have less control over their cognition followed by feelings or emotions. We exercise the least control over physiology. Consequently, ascending from physiology to actions, the efficacy of choosing increases. As 12 step programs teach, "It is easier to act your way to a new way of thinking than it is to think your way to a new way of acting." Conceptualizing behavior as including thinking and feelings adds a dimension to the definition of behavior. Traditionally, the term *behavior* is synonymous with actions, but for the purpose of appreciating the interdependence and the energizing nature of each element, Glasser has coined the phrase *total behavior*, grouping actions, cognition, emotions, and physiology together as a unit.

To further illustrate the energizing nature of behavior, it is helpful to describe the components of total behavior not as static conditions but as having an element of vigor contained in them. Consequently, a person is not described as depressed but as "depress-ing," not as angry but as "anger-ing," not as shamed but "shame-ing." The word *choice* empowers clients to see their feelings as controllable rather than out of control. Sharf (2008) accurately observes, "Glasser believes when people say 'I am choosing to depress' rather that 'I am depressed' they are less likely to choose to depress and therefore less likely to feel depressed" (p. 378).

Throughout the therapy process, reality therapists assist clients to change their actions as well as their thinking. They use the principles described above with empathy, circumspection, and caution. Clinical experience has shown that clients are not helped by a precipitous and reckless education about "choosing your behavior." As with all therapy theories and methods, well-timed interventions based on a firm therapeutic alliance are central to a client's decision to alter behavior resulting in improved mental health.

Another useful analogy for understanding total behavior and for teaching it to clients, parents, or students in a school setting is the reality therapy car. Figure 3.3 illustrates total behavior as well as the motivational system. The front wheels of the car are acting and thinking; the rear wheels are feelings and physiology. When steering, a driver has more control over the front wheels, and when the wheels are turned, the entire car follows. The needs provide the driving force for the car, and the wants provide the specific direction. When the car runs as it should, each component functions as an integral part of a system. For example, the back wheels of the car, though less directly controlled, often indicate that the system has been disrupted. Physical pain tells us that something is wrong. Emotional pain such as "depress-ing," "anger-ing," "anxiety-ing," "panic-ing," "phobic-ing," "obsess-ing," and "paranoid-ing" are signals sent to the driver of the car that something is wrong and action is required. The action to be taken, from a psychological point of view, is a change in the overall direction, specific actions (front wheels), or an alteration in wants.

Total Behavior: Case Example

Lee, male, 38, referred by a coworker, seeks therapy because he was rejected 7 months ago by his girlfriend of 6 years. He discloses that he has been unable to sleep properly, that his appetite is suppressed, and that when he does eat, he eats "comfort food" such as pastries, sweets, and starch. Additionally, he suffers from headaches, lower back pain, and chronic upset stomach. His emotions vary from a state of "down in the dumps" to anger at himself for having lost his "ideal mate." He is afraid to face friends and neighbors because of the embarrassment and shame. He spends hours each day asking himself such questions as, "Why did this happen to me?" "What did I do wrong?" "Why didn't she tell me earlier about what she didn't like about me?" "Was there another man?" "What can I do to get her back?" "Nothing seems to work." He spends hours watching television but is unaware of what he has seen. On the weekends he sits in his house with the drapes drawn, waiting in vain for her to call. He admits that he is drinking too much and that his performance at work has been suffering. His manager has discussed his productivity with him several times and has warned him that change is necessary if he is to remain employed.

Figure 3.3   Total Behavior

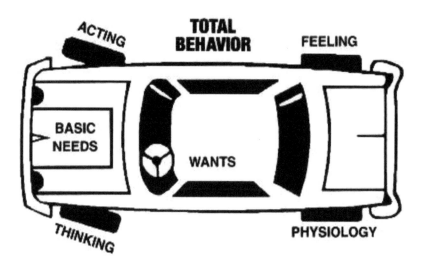

Lee's suitcase of behavior is clearly seen in this example. His physiology requires a medical assessment. His emotions also send him a signal that his life is heading out of control. Indulging in repetitious negative self-talk prevents him from taking effective charge of his life. However and most importantly, he has more control over his actions than the other components of behavior. Using the analogy of the behavioral car (see Figure 3.3), the reality therapist observes that the back wheels, physiology and emotions, are the most prominent evidence of ineffective living. Lee is depress-ing about his loss, anxiety-ing about his career, anger-ing about his mistakes, shame-ing and embarrass-ing about his poor judgment regarding his former girlfriend, jealousy-ing about a phantom rival, fear-ing social situations, and worry-ing about his alcohol consumption.

Operationally a therapist has many starting points. Dealing with physiology, a medical assessment is in order, as well as a possible psychiatric evaluation to determine if medication is needed. The reality therapist would acknowledge the feelings but would not see them as the source of Lee's actions. Rather, they accompany his actions. The therapy process would focus on the front wheels of his behavioral car, with the aim of assisting him to change his actions and secondarily his self-talk. This case will be discussed further under the reality therapy procedures section.

PURPOSE OF BEHAVIOR

Similar to Adlerian theory and practice (Carlson & Englar-Carlson, 2008), choice theory includes the principle that behavior is purposeful or goal directed. The two-fold purpose of behavior, as illustrated by two arrows in Figure 3.2, is to impact the external world and to communicate with it.

Impacting the External World

Human beings choose their actions and implicitly change the other components of total behavior for the purpose of molding and maneuvering their environment to gain the perception of satisfying their needs. Using the analogy of the suitcase, we lift it by its handle and carry it in a direction toward a destination. The analogy of the automobile means driving the vehicle intentionally and purposefully. The importance of defining wants and desires and clarifying them becomes crucial to enhancing mental health. If clients have not refined and illuminated their wants, the resulting behavior seems random, confused, and miscalculated. The disordered behavioral car travels chaotically.

For instance, a mentally healthy person seeks a relationship, selects caring and supportive behaviors toward another person, and respects his or her decision to be mutually engaging or to disengage. A person choosing ineffective behaviors opts for behaviors characterized by self-centeredness, narcissism, overdependence, or even hostility.

The second purpose of behavior is to send a message or signal to the world around us. Human behavior communicates a message, sometimes intended and sometimes unintended. People observing others' behavior receive information, a communiqué, not only about their behavior but about their wants, perceptions, and needs, either satisfied or unsatisfied. Actions and physiology provide concrete and detailed messages. The cognition and emotions accompanying these two specific behaviors also deliver a message. Persons characterized by effective mental health demonstrate at least *some* congruence and appropriateness between their wants and behavior as a communication system. Someone seeking a relationship maintains a suitcase with assertive, courteous, and considerate behavioral communication tools. A person given to ineffective behaviors extracts from the suitcase counterproductive communication methods. For instance, an adolescent wanting to be "left alone" often chooses behaviors that send a message encouraging adults to impose even more restrictions.

The two-fold purpose of behavior underscores the gravity of therapists' efforts to assist clients to clarify their blurred pictures of what they want, to describe their behavior, and to conduct a fearless self-evaluation of the effectiveness and appropriateness of it from a personal and societal point of view, followed by efficacious planning. For example, rebellious teenagers would clarify exactly what it means to "be left alone" and to "have people off my back and not telling me what to do." They would describe the exact connection between their goal or want and their actions. Therapists would then ask them if the people around them are getting the hoped-for message and whether hostile behavior increases or decreases their personal freedom. These self-evaluation questions precede the formulation of realistic doable alternative plans. In other words, they implement choice theory by practicing the WDEP system of reality therapy—that is, exploring wants, doing (total behavior), self-evaluation, and planning.

PERCEPTUAL SYSTEM

Human beings generate behaviors for the general purpose of gaining input from their external worlds. The information provided by the environment is stored in the perceptual system, which is divided into two parts: perceived world and levels of perception.

Perceived World

Analogous to a file cabinet containing memories, current viewpoints, and, in general, our worldview, the perceived world houses perceptions viewed as pleasurable or positive, painful or negative, and neutral. For instance, we have childhood memories that evoke pleasure as well as recollections that might be painful to consider. Current perceptions of people, places, things, ideas, and other information are judged as need-satisfying while others are seen as assaulting the quality world and need system. The goal of the therapist is sometimes to help clients change their perceptions from painful to less painful and even neutral.

Levels of Perception

As illustrated in Figure 3.2, information from the outside world is received and filtered through several lenses or levels of perception. Glasser (1984, 2005b) posits two levels of perception. The lower level functioning as a lens or screen allows information to enter the perceived world and simply labels it. The person sees the information without judging it. When someone walks into a room and sees a chair, it is simply categorized: chair. No judgment is made about its value. This filter is known by various names: recognition filter, low level of perception filter, or total knowledge filter in that we simply know and recognize the world at this level of perception (Glasser, 2005b).

The second level of perception, called the valuing or high level of perception filter, serves as a lens for placing a value on incoming information. The value could be positive, negative, or neutral as when it passed through the low-level filter. Someone observes a chair that has been in the family for generations. The person places a positive value on this treasured family heirloom. On the other hand, a person visiting a state penitentiary is shown the electric chair. This piece of furniture has a nondesirable or high negative value.

Wubbolding (2000a, 2009a) has added a third level of perception—the relationship filter or the middle level of perception. At this level we make connections that precede the subsequent positive or negative valuing placed on incoming information. The following riddle provided by Ken Lyons of The William Glasser Institute Ireland illustrates the need for adding a third level of perception to choice theory: A physician arrives as a guest at a lawn party. The host pours her a small beverage. Immediately her cell phone rings; there's an emergency at the hospital. She rapidly swallows her drink and rushes to the hospital where she provides medical help for a few hours. She then returns to the party to discover the guests lying dead on the ground. Because of her experience as a skilled physician, she instantly determines that the guests have been poisoned.

Question: Why did she not die? *Answer:* The poison was in the ice.

This riddle contains all the facts. The physician not only recognizes corpses (low level of perception) but sees the corpses from a high level of perception and places a negative value on this event. Additionally, because of her sharpened middle level of perception, she sees the relationship between the deaths themselves and their cause. Clearly, human beings not only label incoming information and put a value on it, they also see connections between events, actions, people, ideas, data, and objects.

This riddle also illustrates another fundamental principle of choice theory: Behavior controls human perception. The accumulation of many behaviors stored in the behavioral suitcase constitutes experience. For example, someone having pleasant experiences with an acquaintance will eventually perceive that person as a desired friend. The principle that behavior or experience controls perceptions contains sociological and cultural implications. Experiencing people different from oneself affects and controls our perceptions of them. Pleasant or need-satisfying experiences result in positive attitudes or perceptions toward persons of a different race, age, and/or gender. On the other hand, painful experiences can result in negative attitudes or perceptions toward them.

Therapeutic applications of this principle for a family therapist include helping family members spend time with each other that is pleasurable and nonthreatening. This shared experience results in each person building a storehouse of perceptions that are need-satisfying and bring family members together. Then they see each other in a more positive manner and are more inclined to insert the other family members into their respective quality worlds.

Functions of Perception

Without denying objective realities, from a psychological point of view perception creates reality. For some people a hard surface soothes their back pain while others prefer a soft mattress. The question arises, "Which is better, soft or hard?" The answer is, "Which do you prefer?" Some find spring more pleasant, while others find autumn more satisfying. Every teacher of adults has discovered questions that require irreconcilable answers. "Is the room comfortable? Is it too hot or too cold?" "Do you prefer lecture or group discussions?" "Are you satisfied with your C grade?" A local news reporter interviewed a man who had a sign on his truck that read, "Pray for snow." The owner, a tow truck driver, told the reporter, "In the winter there is no substitute for slush. Some see slush, we see gravy."

An umpire creates reality. The story is told about a 1920s National League umpire, Bill Clem, who was known for long pauses before calling pitches balls or strikes. In one game after several innings, an impatient pitcher yelled at him, "Is it a ball or a strike?" The umpire's answer was, "It ain't nothin' til I calls it somethin'." Human perception is an umpire. It serves as an arbiter. This is not to deny that it can be proven erroneous. A videotape of a baseball play often demonstrates the erroneous judgment of the umpire. Nevertheless, the umpire's final judgment creates the reality regardless of the lingering opinion of the opposing coach and fans.

In addition, perception can create an inner reality. Wubbolding (2000a) relates an incident that occurred while he taught in Japan:

> I witnessed a participant, Yoki Nasada, illustrate how perception creates (inner) reality. She asked ten people in the group to close their eyes and extend their hands forward with their palms up. She stated,

"In the right hand you have a thick phone book. It is heavy, very heavy. As you hold the book, it seems to get even heavier. Tied to your left hand are five balloons, all lighter than air. These balloons are light so light that they seem to want to float higher and higher into the air." She continued this same theme for approximately two minutes. Upon opening our eyes, we discovered that the hand with the imaginary phone book had sunken lower than the opening position and the hand with the balloons was noticeably elevated. I personally report that I felt the hand with the phone book get heavier and sink involuntarily as if it had a heavy weight on it. Our brains chose to perceive an experience and our perception created a reality. (p. 24)

Behavior as purposeful and as a communication system is an attempt to mold or shape the world around us so that we gain specific perceptions matching our wants. Human beings want the perception of having a relationship with a specific person and desire reciprocal affection satisfying the need for belonging. We seek a satisfying job fulfilling the need for power. The perception of humor satisfies a want related to fun or enjoyment. Even the anticipation of a relaxing weekend satisfies the need for freedom. The insidiousness of drugs is that human beings can gain the perception of satisfying their quality worlds and needs with little effort. People seek satisfying perceptions and the maintenance of these perceptions even to the degree of blocking incoming information. Parents sometimes do not want to hear what their adult children did when they were teenagers. Many individuals would rather not see the horror of torture or warfare or even violent movies.

Case Example

From its beginning in a mental hospital and a correctional institution, reality therapy has been applied in multicultural settings. Training institutes exist in many countries in which indigenous psychologists, counselors, and social workers apply the WDEP principles to a wide range of clients. In North America professional therapists reach out to clients from populations characterized by ethnicity, religion, race, sexual orientation, or age.

The case below illustrates the use of reality therapy with a client differing in many ways from her therapist. Carmen, a 23-year-old, U.S. citizen whose parents migrated from Mexico, was recently released from prison where she had served 3 years for drug-related crimes, including robbery. During her prison term, she completed her GED and received her high school equivalency certificate. Upon release from prison, Carmen was placed in a half-way house for women. She has a history of gang-related involvement and first encountered the legal system at age 15 because of serious antisocial behavior. She is now court ordered to receive psychotherapy.

She plans to live with her mother, who has a reputation for being a "trouble maker" in the community and who is seen by case workers as enabling her daughter to avoid responsibility for her behavior. Both Carmen and her mother see themselves as victims discriminated against by an oppressive and unjust society. They ascribe prejudice and bigotry to business owners in their community, educational institutions, and the criminal justice system. They point to the disproportionate number of minority school dropouts and overrepresentation in the criminal justice system. Carmen has repeatedly stated, "The only way to deal with *them* is my way, not their way." The court has assigned an experienced therapist, a White male in his 40s, to work with her and to help her remain free of drugs and free of further involvement in the criminal justice system. More specifically, the court has directed the therapist to "motivate Carmen to find legitimate employment and to acquire crime free relationships."

From the point of view of the therapist, the diversity challenge includes understanding and dealing with possible cultural values based on ethnicity, gender, age, and social class. As if this were not daunting enough, the therapist must also deal with the culture of the court—that is, the judge's expectations, and finally with values and behaviors seen as central to effective mental health. These latter values and behaviors might or might not coincide with the complexities of Carmen's current situation, especially her view of the correctional system and its mandates. The therapist will help her express and clarify her attitudes toward the court and toward what is regarded by the mental health profession as positive and productive living.

Carmen's reality therapist conceptualizes her situation from several points of view and on various levels. He is willing to work within the limitations and expectations of the court system as well as the standards established by the mental health agency. Consequently, some of the goals are predetermined and imposed. Practicing reality therapy, however, allows for wide latitude in establishing intermediate goals and objectives. The therapist's goals can be seen as focusing on the court's expectations, mental health goals (i.e., satisfaction of needs), and process goals such as helping Carmen evaluate her behavior and make more effective plans.

Below are sample dialogues between the therapist and Carmen. These represent possible questions and responses while omitting the usual pleasantries that occur in any relationship. These interactions represent the use of reality therapy rather than issues focusing on informed consent, limitations of confidentiality, and duty to warn. Reality therapists embrace standard practice and function according to ethical principles. Consequently, the dialogue that follows is limited to that which typifies the use of reality therapy.

Therapist: Carmen, now that we've reviewed the standard ethical issues in mental health counseling, I'd like to ask you how you feel about being here.

Client: I don't know why I'm here. This is just more of the same bull . . . that people lay on me.

Therapist: It sounds like the last thing you want to do is come here and talk to a psychological therapist.

Client: Yeah, I talked to shrinks in prison. All they do is say, "Uh huh" and give me some kind of a diagnosis so they can write it in their report.

Therapist: So, you don't believe you got any help from them? That would be pretty aggravating. I can see why you're upset about coming back for what might be more of the same.

Client: That's right. Nuthin's ever happened from these sessions.

Therapist: So you agree with what I just said?

Client: Yeah.

Therapist: Actually, what I did say was these conversations *might* be more of the same. What if these sessions were different from what you've experienced in the past?

Client: I don't see how they could be different. What do you know about me? I don't believe you've got anything to offer me.

Therapist: Well, let's talk about why I'm *unable* to help you. I'm older than you, I'm a man, and I'm White. How do you feel about talking to somebody like this?

Client: You're part of the White, male, power-hungry crowd that tries to deny minorities what they have coming to them.

Therapist: I won't argue with you about that point, but here you are talking to me and you seem to be very frank and honest with me. I'm surprised that you feel comfortable enough to be so open about how you feel.

Client: You ain't heard nuthin' yet.

Therapist: You might want to tell me, but let's come back to that point. I want to ask you some other questions; nothing too personal. I'm wondering what you think about all of these people making demands of you: police, court, probation officer, a future employer, the staff at the half-way house, even your mother whom you hope to live with.

Client: My mother's okay. But I don't have a problem. What right do all these White people have to tell me what to do?

Therapist: So, all the people telling you what to do are White?

Client: They might as well be.

Therapist: They're ordering you around and telling you what to do. Here is a very important question. What do these individuals want from you?

Client: They want me to do what they want: keep their stupid rules.

Therapist: You said before, "You ain't heard nuthin' yet." I'd like to hear more. Tell me about it.

Client: If you were raised in a family like mine, you'd know. My old man left us and I'm glad he's gone. I hate his guts. My mother did a lot of things to get money to support us.

Commentary

At this point Carmen describes at length her childhood and adolescence. She says she feels further abused by teachers, law enforcement, and the court system. The therapist listens empathically, but he also listens for and reflects on successes and choices that resulted in positive and fulfilling outcomes.

Therapist: As I listen to you, Carmen, I hear a couple of themes. One is about some nasty people you've met and how they've tried to hurt you. I also heard about several people such as your mother who did everything she could to look out for you. But most especially I heard the story of your determination and your relentless effort to satisfy something deep inside of you: what we call a need for freedom or independence.

Client: You heard right. I don't like people telling me what to do and taking advantage of me.

Therapist: I see that as a real strength and we can talk a lot about that. Right now I'd like to ask you about your future and where you go from here. I see several choices. You've put up with a lot and now you can go down the road of continuing to be upset about what other people have done to you, or you could leave some of the upsetness behind and not let it control you now or in the future. It seems to me you are standing at a fork in the road. One path is misery and one is happiness.

Client: I sure know about misery: too many people telling me what to do and how to live.

Therapist: For instance, the judge wants you to get a job and stay off drugs.

Client: Yeah. What I do is none of his business.

Therapist: Maybe not, but he made it his business. I have a question for you. Would you say that with all these people on your case, you're happy or you're unhappy? Which one?

Client: I don't have a problem.

Therapist: That's why I asked you if you're on the happy road or the misery road, not if you have a problem.

Client: Of course I'm miserable. Wouldn't you be?

Therapist: You bet I would. I'm very lucky. I hardly have anybody telling me what to do. Well, my boss does tell me when to come to work and many other details. But I don't have a probation officer and I've never been in prison.

Client: Then how in the hell are you going to help me? You've never been in prison or took drugs? And you say you can help me?

Therapist: Carmen, that's exactly why I can help you. I am an expert in how to stay off drugs and how to stay out of prison. I also know how to keep judges off my back.

Client: You got it made. You're a White man.

Therapist: That makes it easier. But I'll bet a few White men are in prison. At any rate, a lot of other people have expectations of you. They want something from you. Now, I want to ask you some other questions. You said you were unhappy, kind of miserable. Do you know anybody who is happy? Somebody who doesn't get in trouble?

Client: Yeah. I have a few relatives who've never been in prison. They're happy. My cousin, Juanita, has a job and she seems happy. She doesn't talk to me.

Therapist: Even though she doesn't talk to you, let's talk about her for a moment. Could you give me a couple examples what she does differently than you do?

Client: She goes to work and spends time with her kids. How boring!

Therapist: Could be. But you said she's happy, and she lives a life different than yours.

Client: That's true.

Therapist: What I'd like to help you do is find some choices that happy people make: people who aren't in trouble, who keep the law and seem to enjoy life. If what they're doing is helping them stay out of trouble, maybe you could learn something from them.

Client: Maybe.

Therapist: Let's put it this way. Is the way you've been living until now helping or hurting you? Getting you in trouble or keeping you out of trouble?

Client: I don't care.

Therapist: But if you did care, what would you say?

Client: If prison is what you mean by trouble, it's hurt me in the past.

Commentary

In this brief dialogue, the therapist tries to establish a friendly, nonargumentative, blame-free, and noncritical atmosphere. He reframes their differences and helps her see their barriers as movable and even helpful. He assists her in making a self-evaluation about her behavior while implying that other behaviors as exemplified by those of her cousin are available to her. Adopting these behaviors is in her self-interest. They will be internally satisfying to her. Thus, the work of the reality therapist involves more that utilizing external consequences as a source of motivation.

Several future sessions will focus on establishing a treatment plan. Included in treatment goals are helping Carmen seek and find legal gainful employment (survival and power); a better relationship with her mother with whom she will live; new friends through church, job, or neighborhood (belonging); and regular attendance at a 12-step program (belonging, power, freedom, fun). Emphasis will be placed on maintaining a trusting relationship—that is, a therapeutic environment. Special focus will be given to helping Carmen self-evaluate her behavior based on internal standards and on rules, court requirements, and possible negative and positive consequences to her choices. This journey rarely happens smoothly. It sometimes entails barriers, detours, resistance, and relapse.

Therapist: Carmen, I get the idea from what you've said that you'd like to be free of people ordering you around.

Client: That's right. I want to be left alone.

Therapist: One of the things that I try to help people with is to establish some goals. In other words define their wants, what they'd like to achieve. What do you think about you and I establishing the goal of getting people off your back?

Client: That sounds like a good idea to me.

Commentary

At first glance the agreed-upon goal is contradictory to the principles of choice theory and reality therapy. As human beings, the only behavior we can control is our own. But the goal of getting others off her back equates with changing other people's behavior. On the other hand, the therapist seeks to ally himself with Carmen on *her* standards, not on his. Her perceived world—the way she sees herself in relation to others—is that of a victim oppressed by people in power. Rather than attempting to blindly apply the principle of controlling only one's own behavior, the therapist accepts her want or goal and will help her focus on behaviors that are controllable—her own. This is an example of the artful rather than rigid, mechanical use of reality therapy.

Therapist: We also talked about the unhappiness or misery that you feel. Could we say that getting rid of some of the misery and upsetness could be another goal?

Client: What do you mean *some*?

Therapist: I don't like to make big promises. How realistic is it to get rid of all misery and be completely happy, especially right away?

Client: Well, I'm tired of the misery, and I'd like it to go away. But, I doubt if all of it will ever go away.

Therapist: I think you're right. There will probably always be some people around you that are hard to get along with. But, are you willing to set the goal of being at least a little happier?

Client: That sounds like a start. And you can help me with that?

Therapist: There's not a doubt in my mind. I can't guarantee anything, but I believe that I can help you. And yet this help does contain an "IF."

Client: I thought so. What's the "IF"?

Therapist: "IF" you are willing to commit to taking some steps down the happiness road. Remember we talked about the fork in the road. It seems to me you are standing at the fork in the road and you have two choices: pursue your goals down the happiness road or give up on them and continue down the misery road, the road of being controlled by all the people you mentioned earlier.

Client: How do I do that?

Therapist: That's what we'll discuss in our sessions together. What I hear in the question, "How do I do that?" is a desire on your part to take some steps. Am I right?

Client: That depends. What steps?

Therapist: We haven't really defined exactly what they are but as we talk they will come up in our conversations. In fact, I think one or other of the ideas emerged already. I asked you if you knew anybody who was not "put upon" by courts and probation officers, etc. You mentioned that your cousin Juanita didn't have people ordering her around. At least she had fewer people telling her what to do than you do. Am I right about that?

Client: Yes. But she's a wimp.

Therapist: A happy wimp? A wimp without a probation officer? A wimp that's not been in jail?

Client: All right, all right. I get your point.

Therapist: What do you think the point is?

Client: I guess the point is that wimps are happier and stay out of trouble.

Therapist: You know, Carmen, you're very quick to put ideas together. Normally I would not be so blunt so quickly. But you don't strike me as being fragile. You've been through a lot. And you obviously have a great deal of strength. I believe this strength will help you get what you want. Of course, I can help you, but I can only help you to function within the law and within the expectations of the court.

Commentary

The therapist has helped Carmen establish a second goal. This goal is quite different than the first in that it is more clearly an internally motivated want. Carmen is asked to evaluate the realistically attainability of this want. Moreover, the structure of the relationship between Carmen and therapist is more precise: Change will occur if Carmen exerts effort. Secondly, the therapist must work within external boundaries established in the real world, the world outside the therapeutic relationship. The therapist is willing to express confidence and yet avoids overpromising the inevitability of a happy outcome.

Up until now, the therapist has tried to establish a firm, friendly, and fair atmosphere. He has been cognizant of the importance of the therapeutic alliance based on hope and realistic expectations. He suggests that together they identify a person whose behaviors can serve as concrete desirable examples of choices that lead down the happiness road. He will help Carmen realize that she need not see Juanita's life as completely desirable but that some of her behaviors are effective and healthy.

Overall, the therapist began with a discussion of Carmen's external world and behaviors that she cannot control. Because of his acceptance of her perceived world, the counseling environment—that is, the therapeutic alliance—is strengthened. She is then willing to gradually discuss her wants and is more likely to take responsibility for future choices and perhaps even her past behaviors. I wish to emphasize again that the dialogue described here consists of specific questions and reflections that demonstrate the essence of reality therapy and choice theory. The progress shown in the dialogue might take a longer period of time with real clients. The purpose of the dialogue is to show the developmental nature of the therapeutic process.

In subsequent sessions illustrated below, the therapist helps Carmen describe her feelings, her thinking (self-talk), and especially her actions. He also teaches her about the choice theory motivational system as well as how to use the WDEP system.

In discussing her feelings, the therapist helps Carmen realize that she is capable of feeling better. In fact at times, she currently feels better.

Therapist: During the last few sessions we've talked about what you want and how to get what you want. How do you feel on the gut level when we discuss the future and the fact that you can avoid prison and other troubles in the future?

Client: I noticed that I felt a little better.

Therapist: So even talking about successful plans changes how you feel. How much better do you think you feel when you discuss the future?

Client: Not much, maybe 10% better.

Therapist: No kidding? Just talking helps you feel that much better! That's sounds like a lot to me.

Commentary

The therapist helps Carmen see that change is possible, and he reframes a slight change into a successful giant step. The goal of such dialogue is to communicate a sense of hope and to indirectly help Carmen see herself not as a victim but as an active agent capable of more effective choices to satisfy her needs.

In assisting Carmen to examine her cognitive behaviors, the therapist helps her identify and evaluate self-talk statements based on choice theory.

Therapist: Carmen, we've talked about a few examples of what is called relapse or backsliding. What thoughts go through your mind now about the times you screwed up?

Client: I was heading in the right direction and I sometimes think, "What's the use? I can't control my actions." I know you've taught me that I choose my actions, but it's hard to accept that I have this internal control that you spoke of.

Therapist: Sometimes you seem to feel powerless, like right now. If you continue to tell yourself that you have no control over your life, where will you end up?

Client: In more trouble, back where I came from.

Therapist: Are you willing to replace those kinds of thoughts with their opposites? I see you nodding your head in agreement. What kind of thinking would be better for you to work on?

Client: I need to tell myself that I have choices and that if I screw up I can do like you told me the song says, "pick myself up, dust myself off, and start all over again."

Therapist: Remember I said the song is not completely accurate because you're not *starting all over again.*

Client: All right, all right. I remember you said to think about "everybody makes mistakes and that's why they have a delete button on a computer."

Commentary

The therapist avoids the toxic behaviors of arguing about Carmen's self-talk or blaming and criticizing her for relapse. Rather, he asks her to self-evaluate her current self-talk about the relapse itself.

As the therapy process develops, Carmen self-evaluates the most controllable part of her behavioral system, her actions. She evaluates choices that led to relapse, as well as choices that replace her ineffective behavior.

Therapist: Carmen, if you continue to hang around the same people and go to the same places and avoid 12-step meetings, is anything going to change in your life?

Client: You keep asking me that and my answer is the same. "No."

Therapist: Do you want to substitute something better?

Client: Yes, but it's very hard.

Therapist: Can you do it alone? You know the saying we talked about earlier, "Only you can do it and you can't do it alone." Do you want to get involved with the 12-step program and with people at your church?

Client: I learned the hard way that I need support.

Therapist: How about going to a 12-step meeting when you leave here? I know a sponsor who will meet you at the door if I call her.

Client: Now?

Therapist: No time like the present. How about it, you've come this far.

Client: You don't give up, do you?

Therapist: That thought has never occurred to me. If you attend the meeting tonight, will it help you or hurt you?

Client: I think I know what you want me to say. It will help. (Carmen agrees and the therapist calls a sponsor who will meet her at the meeting).

Therapist: I must confess, I do like to hear that from you. But more importantly, I think you mean it. If you get involved with people at the 12-step program and at your church, what impact will this have on your life?

Client: Judging from what we've talked about during these many sessions, these kinds of relationships will replace those that have taken me down. We also talked about how these relationships will provide me with enjoyment and fun that does not lead me back to that miserable judge.

Therapist: One last comment before you go. In the beginning of the counseling process, you said that it might be difficult for you to talk to me and for me, a White man, older than you to be able to help you. What do you think now?

Client: Truthfully, you're not so bad.

Therapist: So it is possible for you to find people, even some of a different race or age, who can help you in your struggle. I think you've proven this to yourself.

Commentary

The therapist emphasizes self-evaluation and helps Carmen review her actions as they connect with the satisfaction of her needs: belonging, power or inner control, freedom or independence, and fun or enjoyment. He helps her reflect on the fact that she can successfully relate to people different from her.

Future Sessions

Future sessions will focus on maintaining Carmen's interpersonal relationships; seeking, securing, and maintaining successful employment; exploring enjoyable leisure activities; and examining the spirituality she experiences at church. In general, as she abandons her destructive lifestyle and progresses, Carmen will encounter new challenges characteristic of productive living. In other words, her success will bring its own problems. The therapy will emphasize clarification and development of specific wants in her quality world as these relate to her five needs. She will examine her behaviors and develop the habit of conducting a fearless, searching, and non-self-critical evaluation of the realistic attainability of her wants and the effectiveness of her choices. She will formulate a map of life with established routines and plans for dealing with unexpected stressors and other blockades on the happiness road. After she has learned the principles of inner motivation derived from choice theory and if she has practiced and learned the WDEP system, Carmen can live a life satisfactory to herself and to those around her.

The case of Carmen illustrates that choice theory explains human behavior: its origin, its components, and its purpose. It is comprehensive, multicultural, and understandable to both professionals and the public. As a universally applicable theory, it serves as the basis for the delivery system reality therapy, and it can be directly taught and understood by clients as well as by students. After describing choice theory as an internal control system, Glasser (1998) states,

> Choice theory is a complete change from what has been common sense to what I hope will become, in time, a new common sense. This change is not easy. It can happen only through learning what is wrong with external control psychology and the overwhelming reasons to replace it with choice theory. (p. 7)

Glasser believes that the destructiveness of attempts to control other people can hardly be overemphasized and that choice theory provides an effective worldview for bringing harmony to family and community relationships.

The editor of the *International Journal of Reality Therapy*, Larry Litwack (2005), in speaking of the growth of choice theory, states, "Over the years I have watched the ideas grow and spread like a giant oak tree. As the oak grows from a single acorn, so the ideas of internal control psychology began to develop" (p. 3). The principles of choice theory as well as the WDEP system of reality therapy are now taught in many countries by indigenous instructors and have been applied to individuals from a wide range of ethnic groups. Consequently, the reason that the ideas are taught throughout the world is that they are not ethnocentric but rather universal, that they are not uniform but adaptable, and that they are not rigid but allow for individual creativity.

4

The Therapy Process

THERAPEUTIC ALLIANCE AND THE WDEP SYSTEM

This chapter discusses the therapeutic process of reality therapy and illustrates how the theory is put into action with case vignettes and examples. I will allude to other theories, pointing out similarities but emphasizing the uniqueness of reality therapy.

A common practice among psychotherapy theorists is establishing a safe atmosphere or environment. The result is that clients can feel free to explore their problems, inner thoughts, and feelings, as well as their personal successes, without fear of criticism. This therapeutic alliance serves as the basis for the therapist's interventions. Theorists also use acronyms to summarize and express both theory and practical interventions. Rational emotive behavioral therapy is known as REBT with its ABCs. Multimodal therapy uses the BASIC-ID. The WDEP formulation (wants, doing, self-evaluation, planning) expresses in a learnable and teachable manner the extension of choice theory as rendered operational in the delivery system reality therapy (Wubbolding, 2008a, 2008b). Glasser and Glasser (2008) accentuate the central place of procedures in theory and practice:

> We wish to state publicly that teaching the procedures, the WDEP system, continues to be an integral part of training participants wishing to learn choice theory and reality therapy . . . this system helps to formulate and deliver questions and offer mental health workers, educators, criminal justice personnel, organizations and others a practical method facilitating solutions that are internally motivational. (p. 1)

When implementing choice theory, reality therapists and clients explore its various components: needs, wants, scales, choice, four components of total behavior, purpose of their behaviors, and perceptions, including how they perceive the world around them. The therapeutic alliance, the relationship between therapists and clients, forms the foundation for successful psychotherapy. In the language of choice theory, therapists become part of the clients' quality worlds; that is, they see the reality therapist as a partner helping them to achieve their goals, empathize with their point of view, and support their efforts. When the therapeutic alliance is strong enough, reality therapists ask clients to reflect on their behavior, evaluate it, and change it.

CREATING THE ENVIRONMENT: THERAPEUTIC ALLIANCE

Establishing a safe but challenging environment requires the conventional skills and personal qualities common to most theories: empathy, congruence, and positive regard. The therapist sees the world from the point of view of the client, possesses communication skills that are both direct and respectful, and maintains an attitude that values the client.

As shown in Figure 4.1, there is no absolute separation between environment and procedures. However, for purposes of learning theory and practice, it is useful to distinguish between these two major components of reality therapy.

Figure 4.1   Cycle of Psychotherapy and Counseling

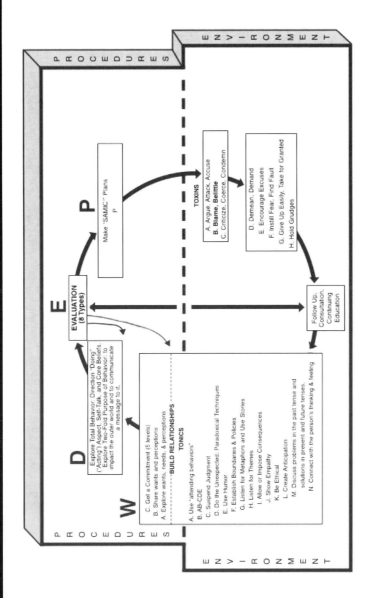

Figure 4.1 *continued*

SUMMARY DESCRIPTION OF THE
CYCLE OF PSYCHOTHERAPY AND COUNSELING

Introduction:

The Cycle consists of two general concepts: Environment conducive to change and Procedures more explicitly designed to facilitate change. This chart is intended to be a **brief** summary.

Relationship between Environment & Procedures:

1. As indicated in the chart, the Environment is the foundation upon which the effective use of Procedures is based.

2. Though it is **usually** necessary to establish a safe, friendly Environment before change can occur, the "Cycle" can be entered at any point. Thus, the use of the cycle does **not** occur in lock step fashion.

3. Building a relationship implies establishing and maintaining a professional relationship. Methods for accomplishing this comprise some efforts on the part of the helper that are Environmental and others that are Procedural.

ENVIRONMENT:
Relationship Tonics:
A. Using Attending Behaviors: Eye contact, posture, effective listening skills.
B. AB = "Always **B**e . . ." Consistent, **C**ourteous & **C**alm, **D**etermined that there is hope for improvement & **E**nthusiastic (Think Positively).
C. Suspend Judgment: View behaviors from a low level of perception, i.e., acceptance is crucial.
D. Do the Unexpected: Use paradoxical techniques as appropriate; Reframing and Prescribing.
E. Use Humor: Help them fulfill need for fun within reasonable boundaries.
F. Establish boundaries: the relationship is professional.
G. Listen for Metaphors: Use their figures of speech and provide other ones. Use stories.
H. Listen to Themes: Listen for behaviors that have helped, value judgements, etc.
I. Allow or Impose Consequences: Within reason, they should be responsible for their own behavior.
J. Show Empathy: Perceive as does the person being helped.
K. Be Ethical: Study Codes of Ethics and their applications, e.g., how to handle suicide threats or violent tendencies.
L. Create anticipation and communicate hope. People should be taught that something good will happen if they are willing to work.
M. Discuss problems in the past tense, solutions in present and future tenses.
N. Connect with the person's thinking and feeling.

Relationship Toxins:

Argue, Blame, Criticize or Coerce, Demean, Encourage Excuses, Instill Fear, or Give up easily, Hold Grudges.

Rather, stress what they **can** control, accept them as they are, and keep the confidence that they can develop more effective behaviors. Also, continue to us "WDEP" system without giving up.

Follow Up, Consult, and Continue Education:

Determine a way for them to report back, talk to another professional person when necessary, and maintain ongoing program of professional growth.

PROCEDURES:
Build Relationships:

WDEP

A. Explore **W**ants, Needs & Perceptions: Discuss picture album or quality world, i.e., set goals, fulfilled & unfulfilled pictures, needs, viewpoints and "locus of control."

B. Share Wants & Perceptions: Tell what you want from them and how you view their situations, behaviors, wants, etc. This procedure is secondary to A above.

C. Get a Commitment: Help them solidify their desire to find more effective behaviors.

Explore Total Behavior:

Help them examine the **D**irection of their lives, as well as specifics of how they spend their time. Discuss core beliefs and ineffective & effective self talk. Explore two-fold purpose of behavior: to impact the outer world and to communicate a message to it.

Evaluation – The Cornerstone of Procedures:

Help them evaluate their behavioral direction, specific behaviors as well as wants, perceptions and commitments. Evaluate own behavior through follow-up, consultation and continued education.

Make **P**lans: Help them change direction of their lives.

Effective plans are **S**imple, **A**ttainable, **M**easurable, **I**mmediate, **C**onsistent, **C**ontrolled by the planner, and **C**ommitted to. The helper is **P**ersistent. Plans can be linear or paradoxical.

From *Theory and Practice of Counseling and Psychotherapy* (8th Ed., p. 110–111), by G. Corey, 2009, Belmont, CA: Thomson Brooks/Cole. Created and copyrighted 1986, 2010 by Robert E. Wubbolding. Reprinted with permission.

Toxic Behaviors

Counterproductive to a firm, fair, and friendly environment are the ABCs that create poisonous relationships. Not only do these damage the therapeutic alliance, they also undermine other human relationships. Arguing increases resistance and un-cooperation. Blaming and belittling worsen guilt and shame. Criticizing, coercing, and demeaning diminish self-esteem and independence. Facilitating and colluding with excuses damages the possibility of behavioral change. Instilling fear results in avoidance of responsibility, increased anger, and resentment. Giving up communicates rejection. Holding grudges renders the grudge holder less attractive to others.

Psychotherapists are not inclined to employ toxic behaviors in their professional demeanor with their clients *as a rule*. However, lacking alternative skills it is not unknown for a neophyte therapist to occasionally resort to such tactics, at least in a mild manner. Additionally, therapists often teach the toxicity of such behaviors when consulting with parents, educators, managers, and supervisors. In his lectures Glasser emphasizes the destructive nature of deadly habits that he enumerates as: criticizing, blaming, complaining, nagging, threatening, punishing, and bribing or rewarding to control. He points out that their habitual use kills relationships.

Tonic Behaviors

The therapeutic relationship is nurtured by reality-centered behaviors initiated by the therapist. Some of these suggestions can be directly taught to clients, both individually and in group therapy, but they are all intended for use by the therapist when deemed helpful. Whenever they are used, they should be employed with the intent to promote a bonding between client and therapist.

Ivey, D'Andrea, Ivey, and Simek-Morgan (2007) describe the importance of "attending behaviors" as a foundational microskill in the therapeutic relationship. Eye contact, facial expression, posture, gestures, verbal following, voice tone, and other nonverbal behaviors communicate an unspoken message of acceptance, tolerance, disapproval, rejection, indifference, shock, and surprise. Cultural differences often dictate appropriate and inappropriate attending behaviors. For example, lack of eye contact is a respectful behavior in some cultures and a defiant behavior for individuals of other cultures. Some individuals see the therapist sitting behind the desk as a person commanding respect and whose opinion carries weight. Others regard this arrangement of furniture as an obstruction between the therapist and themselves as well as a roadblock to progress.

AB-CDE represents suggestions for therapists for use with clients as well as ideas for teaching alternatives to toxic behaviors: Always Be Courteous, Determined, and Enthusiastic. Following guidelines regarded as courteous hardly requires training for therapists. However, for clients to incorporate seemingly self-evident polite behaviors often takes encouragement, practice, and considerable discussion about the purpose and possible results of what sometimes feels like a new and creative choice. The effective reality therapist demonstrates and communicates a sense of determination—a belief that clients can improve their lives. For example, a therapist attempting to be empathic by reflecting on clients' powerlessness and misery often communicates a sense of hopeless victimhood. Using the WDEP system, however, helps clients move beyond the feeling of being immobilized and trapped in their despondency. They see the hopefulness and willingness of the therapist to help them, and they come to believe that they can climb out of the pit of desolation or at least discomfort. Enthusiasm does not equate with cheerleading but rather entails a cooperative and relentless search for successes and positive aspects of the client's story. An alcoholic of many years mentions that he was sober for 6 months 5 years ago. The therapist sees this as a genuine accomplishment requiring heroic effort, not merely a break in a career of defeat.

Other behaviors helpful in establishing and maintaining the environment of the therapeutic alliance include suspending judgment, employing paradoxical techniques when appropriate, doing the unexpected, maintaining a sense of humor, clarifying boundaries, and using metaphors. Reality therapists develop the art of listening, but it does not serve the exclusive purpose of relationship building. It also facilitates the empowerment of the client in that the therapist listens for themes as well as summarizing them and focusing on issues related to the WDEP system, such as:

- What the client wants from family, friends, job, school, therapist, and, most importantly, from himself or herself;
- What the client has been doing, thinking, and feeling about himself or herself and, his or her wants and goals and about the people around him or her; and
- Whether the client's wants are attainable and whether his or her actions, thinking, and feelings are helpful (self-evaluation).

Other tools for maintaining a quality relationship include appropriate silence, accurate empathy, and the creation of a sense of anticipation. From the very beginning of the relationship, clients realize that something is going to happen, that this therapy is not mere talk. It is action centered. They come to realize that the therapist believes that problems are in the past and solutions are in the present. The therapist communicates this belief through the language and grammar used. For example, "You had this problem in the past. Would you now want to choose to leave it there and to replace it with something better?" The endless discussion of their personal history or issues over which they have no control only serves to keep them anchored in a condition of stagnation.

Establishing the therapeutic alliance, the connection between therapist and client, proceeds at a different pace with each person. Some clients feel instant rapport with a reality therapist, while others require more proof that the helper is truly a helper. For example, a hostile client of a lower economic level group might initially perceive a middle economic level therapist as part of the oppressive system preventing him or her (the client) from achieving freedom and independence. Consequently, building trust can be an arduous and even painful task.

INTERVENING WITH REALITY THERAPY PROCEDURES: THE WDEP SYSTEM

Many of the skills for establishing a constructive atmosphere in the therapeutic relationship are common to other theories and are characteristics of healthy human relationships. Consequently, they serve as an appropriate foundation for reality therapy interventions based on choice theory. Most typical of reality therapy is a systematic series of interventions summarized by the acronym WDEP (Wubbolding, 1989, 1991, 2000a, 2008c). Each letter represents a cluster of possible ways to help clients become increasingly aware of the various elements of their internal control systems, examine a broader spectrum of opportunities, and thereby make more effective choices. These four letters focus the theory on clinical practice and provide its delivery system, making it usable for the therapist and for the client. In speaking of the WDEP system, Glasser stated, "It is an eminently usable tool that can be learned by readers, used in agencies and schools, and taught in classrooms. I hope that this system will become a household phrase and used by therapists, counselors, teachers and parents (Wubbolding, 1991, p. xii).

EXPLORING WANTS

The key question under the W of the WDEP system is:

WHAT DO YOU *WANT?*

The user of reality therapy is aware of the theoretical concept of the quality world. Its contents are everything highly valued: core beliefs, ideas, and treasured possessions and relationships. The question, "What do you want?" summarizes quality world interventions made by the therapist. The Appendix *Exploring Wants* further details more than 100 possible inquiries for both client and therapist to explore and ponder for future planning. In exploring the quality world, the therapist assists clients to formulate, clarify, and prioritize the pictures in their mental picture albums—that is, their wants. This process serves as the foundation for other interventions based on the WDEP system and requires much attention in the therapeutic process. Its importance is illustrated in the well-known caution to "be careful what you wish for." An employee desiring early retirement might be well advised to avoid nurturing "medical retirement" as a quality world picture. This desire might result not in the satisfaction of the freedom need; it might result in a threat to the survival need.

Levels of Wants

Because of the primary importance of wants, the quality world is often referred to as the "world of wants." Though rich in content, the common denominator of the various ingredients of the quality world—and therefore the focus of therapy—consists in the *wants* of the client. Everything in the quality world appears desirable. However, these wants are not constant or standardized. They exist at various levels of desirability and are changeable.

- *Nonnegotiable demand*. Some wants, such as the desire for oxygen, nourishment, or the freedom from torture, are so intensely desired that clients cannot function without them. Some clients rigidly cling to wants that, in fact, damage relationships. However, with skillful counseling and negotiation, clients can move toward more fluid wants and better relationships. For example, an unyielding parent insists that an adolescent conform to the same rules that were in force during childhood.
- *Pursued goal*. Clients expressing the positive symptom "I want to improve" formulate goals that are backed up by behaviors. Going to school, developing a positive relationship, finding a job, joining a 12-step program are examples. A more intense want could replace a pursued goal as when a young person enlists in military service and leaves behind a relationship.
- *Wish*. Some effort is made to achieve the wish, but its satisfaction requires little exertion. Taking a chance on the lottery entails less than overwhelming effort. Sometimes a wish focuses on something impossible to achieve. A resident of northern Minnesota might wish for Caribbean-like weather in January or a resident of Jamaica might wish for snow to practice tobogganing for the Winter Olympics.
- *Weak whim*. Fulfilling this want is slightly desirable but of little importance. A man selects a tie to wear for work but cares little about the exact

color or design. In counseling couples, one person expresses the pursued goal of a happier relationship, while the other says that it would be nice but it is of little value.

- *Double bind.* Sabotaging a want with ineffective behaviors sends the signal, "I want it but I don't want it." A person genuinely wants to lose weight but undermines the effort by consistently overeating. Habitual bickering in a relationship damages the achievement of a genuine want expressed by couples, "We want our marriage to improve."
- *Reluctant passive acceptance.* Clients on their own or through therapy learn to accept the inevitable. While not desired, many people gain an acceptance of a disease, handicap, situation, or event. A person feels pain at rejection by a lover. Someone contracts a fatal illness or is injured in an accident. Another person experiences a loss of physical prowess or even faces death. Though the unavoidable may be undesirable, human beings learn to accept it.
- *Nondesired active acceptance.* People often formulate clearly defined wants knowing that a side effect or consequence of its fulfillment will be an undesirable result. The pain of childbirth is hardly desirable, yet women accept it as an unavoidable corollary of the joy of giving birth. A battered woman living in a shelter desires to visit her father, knowing that there is a high likelihood of being abused. These side effects are not quality world pictures, but they unavoidably accompany the highly desired want.
- *Fantasy dream.* Even though there is overwhelming evidence that the attainment of the dream is impossible, a person might fantasize about having a family like the Cosby TV family or the Brady Bunch. These wants are out of reach, unattainable, but they remain expressed as "Wouldn't it be nice?"

Though it is not necessary to categorize precisely every want during the process of therapy, it is useful to help clients determine the degree of intensity of a want. Helpful questions include, "How intensely do you want it?" "Is your want a nonnegotiable desire or a weak whim?" "Is it something you intend to pursue relentlessly, or is it something 'it would be nice to have'?" From the perspective of choice theory, the quality worlds of some clients lack priorities among wants. For many people recovering from addictions and members of codependent families, all wants appear to be equally important and urgent. A major part of the reality therapy process with such individuals entails helping them realize that some wants are of greater consequence than others.

Level of Commitment

Asking clients questions focusing on how hard they want to work at achieving their goals or how much energy they wish to exert to satisfy their wants and needs helps them move from Stage I "I want to improve" to Stage II "Positive symptoms" (Figure 4.1). When clients decide that behavioral change is to their advantage, they are ready to make more effective choices and therapy can proceed more rapidly when therapists help them raise their level of commitment. Wubbolding (2000a) has identified five levels of commitment.

1. *"I don't want to be here. Leave me alone. Get off my back."* Clients coerced to attend therapy sessions by family or court often display resistance, reluctance, and even hostility toward change and toward the therapist. This level, in fact, represents no commitment. Yet it is commonly heard by private practitioners, probation officers, child care workers, and practitioners in university counseling centers when clients have experienced an intervention and are *sent* to receive help.

2. *"I want the outcome, but I don't want to make the effort."* Some clients seek better relationships with family members, a job promotion, weight reduction, freedom from oversight by law enforcement, or a myriad of other wants. Failing to exert effort places their behavior at this second level of commitment. Though slightly higher than the first level, it contains resistance to action planning. The reality therapist helps clients evaluate this level of commitment and its lack of efficacy in effecting want and need fulfillment.

3. *"I'll try." "I might." "I could." "Maybe." "Probably."* The middle level of commitment shows some willingness to take more effective control of one's own behavior. However, change is not immutably linked to an "I'll try" commitment. "Trying" allows room for excuses

and failure. The reality therapist can point to an airline customer's question, "When does your flight leave for Los Angeles?" If the ticket agent responds, "We will try to depart at 9:15 a.m.," the customer would ask for a higher level of commitment. Still, the middle level of commitment represents more resolve than levels 1 or 2.

4. *"I will do my best."* Though containing an escape hatch to failure expressed as "I did my best, but I didn't follow through," doing one's best points toward action planning. It represents a step beyond mere wanting and trying and a willingness to choose positive symptoms.

5. *"I will do whatever it takes."* Efficacious choices and follow-through behaviors characterize the highest level of commitment. Clients consistently follow through on plans and even accept the responsibility for less than desired outcomes. For instance, an employee chooses behaviors designed to ensure a promotion. However, the employer does not bestow the honor desired by the worker. The employee makes no excuses, places no blame, and looks to the future.

The levels of commitment are best seen as developmental. Even though level 3 is not as efficacious as level 5, it can represent a client's improvement in that he or she has moved from resistance and apathy to a higher level of motivation for change.

Exploring Perceptual System

Contained in the perceptual system are two components. Three perceptual filters comprise the first component, whereby human beings acknowledge the world, see relationships, and place a value on incoming information. The second component is the perceived world, a storehouse of perceptions of self and the external world.

When discussing the three perceptual filters, the therapist seeks information and clarification for ascertaining how clients see the world around them. To what degree do they see the world without putting a value on their perceptions? What do they believe is high value for them? Do they see a relationship between how their own behavior impacts the world around them and the incoming information received from it? For example, does a client perceive any connection between treating coworkers rudely and the perception that they don't like him? Does a specific client believe that her use of drugs has a relationship to her loss of family, loss of job, or loss of status? How much does a client value effective, altruistic, or legal behaviors purposely chosen to satisfy needs? Or does the client see value only in behaviors that are an attempt to satisfy needs regardless of whether they are unsuccessful, harmful to others, or even outside the law?

Connected with this exploration is the discussion of locus of control. First formulated by the social learning theorist Rotter (1954), the notions of internal place of control versus a sense of external control coincides with the principles of internal control psychology, more specifically choice theory. In speaking of Rotter's work, Mearns (2008) states,

> People with a strong internal locus of control believe that the responsibility for whether or not they get reinforced lies within themselves. Internals believe that success or failure is due to their own efforts. In contrast, externals believe that the reinforcers in life are controlled by luck, chance or powerful others. Therefore, they see little impact of their own efforts on the amount of reinforcement they receive. (p. 4)

The single difference between Rotter's principle and choice theory is that in choice theory the payoff for behavior is not seen as reinforcing but rather as satisfying the internal motivation, or general needs and specific wants.

Reality therapists help clients ascertain their perceived degree of internal vs. external control. People depress-ing themselves believe that they are at the mercy of external circumstances, that they are powerless because of events beyond their control. Others adopt the self-talk, "I can't because they won't let me." Consequently, one of the goals of reality therapy is to help clients change their perception of victimization by changing their actions. The principle of internal control entails application beyond psychology and therapy. Burnett (1995) states that society is "tired of people claiming to be a victim every time someone confronts them for an antisocial behavior" (p. i). He provides the example of Bart Simpson: "I didn't do it." "Nobody saw me do it." And finally, "You can't prove anything."

Embracing the principle of internal control rather than external control does not imply that every limitation, problem, defeat, or pathology is within a person's ability to control. Many assaults from the external world are unavoidable and are direct attacks against one or more human need: self-preservation, belonging, power or inner control, freedom, and fun. When threatened, it is often difficult and sometimes impossible to generate a need-satisfying behavior. The driver of a car skidding out of control on an icy street is likely to *feel* out of control and unable to choose a relaxed, calm, and self-confidence-ing behavior. Choice theory does not teach that changing perceptions from external to internal is easy, nor is the perception of internal control easily accessible. Therefore, a principle of internal control congruent with choice theory is: *Human beings (clients) have more control than they often perceive.*

If some clients are extreme in their denial of all responsibility, perceive that they are powerless, and contend that change is impossible, others cling to the perception that they are to blame for their own errors and even for the faults of others. They feel excessive shame and guilt, are often overly conscientious and scrupulous to the point of perceiving themselves as worthless, irredeemable sinners. These diagnosable behaviors occupy opposite extremes of the internal/external control continuum.

Choice theory is compatible with Rotter's caution that human beings, for the most part, are a mixture of internal and external control perceptions. Because of this, an appropriate reality therapy question focusing on the perceived locus of control is, "How much of the misery or problem do you believe you are causing yourself?" Regardless of the amount of internal control perceived by the client, the skilled reality therapist can use the answer to facilitate a new perception for the client. If the client responds by insisting he or she has no responsibility, the therapist can reply, "If you haven't caused any of your problems, then anything you do differently will be a step in the right direction." If the client takes too much responsibility or blames himself or herself, the therapist could reply, "I believe I can help you by assisting you to leave some of the misery in this office." These responses do not necessarily bring about immediate improvement, but they are intended to communicate a sense of hope and to encourage the client to believe that more efficacious choices are available—that is, to realize they have more control than they previously believed.

In helping clients move from a sense of external control or victimization to the perception that they have at least some control and that choices are available to them, the use of metaphors can be eye opening. Rather than perceiving a depression as an enemy, a client might be encouraged to see it as a friend accompanying him or her on the road of life. But on the road of life, there are rest stops where a friend can spend some time without accompanying the client. Rather than fighting the obsession and drawing attention to it, a client might put the obsession in a backpack and carry it on the outside rather than in his or her gut. Rather than arguing with a client who refuses to take any responsibility for his or her plight, the reality therapist might discuss the client as feeling like a floor mat and ask, "Would you like to get off the floor and sit in a chair for a while?"

Using metaphors with clients in this manner externalizes the problem, making it more manageable. This process helps clients see choices previously unknown and come to the life-changing realization that they are more in control than previously perceived. The value of this step in their journey can hardly be overestimated.

The W of the WDEP system includes an exploration of the quality world, the wants. The reality therapist listens carefully for expressed or implied wants and asks specific questions about them. How clients see themselves in the world, what they value, what connections they make between their behavior and their perceptions, how they perceive locus of control, and how much change they believe is possible—these and other perceptions constitute part of the W. In addition to careful listening and questioning, the therapist uses metaphors, themes, and careful language focused on internal control when applying the W of the WDEP system.

EXPLORING DOING, OR TOTAL BEHAVIOR

Throughout the course of therapy, clients describe the various components of their total behavior: physiology, emotions, thinking, and actions. At various times some level of the behavioral suitcase or wheel of the car needs more intense scrutiny than the other components. Because actions are more explicitly chosen, most discussion centers on them. Yet, this emphasis does not exclude conversation about the other three components of total behavior.

Physiology

Reality therapists follow the standard practice of responding to physical abuse, injury, and pain. They discuss physical symptoms as appropriate and especially their link to mental health. The therapist's awareness of pain symptoms, real or imagined, helps him or her decide on the degree of immediacy for a referral to a medical professional. Some such symptoms accompany feelings of distress and depression and impede social or occupational functioning, which are more the province of psychotherapy.

Emotions or Feelings

Emotions are seen not as static conditions but as purposeful behaviors generated to impact the external world or to send it a signal. Thus "-ing" words are used to illustrate the lively nature of all feelings. Reality therapists acknowledge feelings and empathize with them but encourage clients to discuss accompanying self-talk and actions.

Cognition or Thinking

Ellis and Harper (1997) and Ellis (2008) have identified self-talk or internal verbalizations related to the underlying principles of rational emotive behavioral therapy. Wubbolding (2000a, 2008c) has extended the practice of reality therapy to include the identification and discussion of cognition related to both ineffective and effective actions.

Ineffective self-talk (IST) includes:

- No one is going to tell me what to do.
- I'm powerless to do anything to change.
- I can control other people.
- Even though my present behavior is not getting me what I want, I will continue to choose it.

Therapeutic interventions focusing on self-talk consist of pinpointing the action accompanying cognition and helping clients to outwardly verbalize it, assisting them to evaluate it with the purpose of replacing it with effective self-talk.

Effective self-talk (EST) includes:

- I am happy when I live within reasonable boundaries.
- I am in control of my actions. I choose my behavior. I can change. I am in charge of my life.
- I cannot control other people's behavior.
- If what I am doing is not helping me, I'll stop doing it and try another course of action.

This conceptualization of self-talk differs from that of rational emotive behavioral therapy and cognitive therapy. From the perspective of choice theory, cognition does not cause actions and is therefore not the cause of effective or ineffective choices. Rather, self-talk *accompanies* actions. All human behavior is composed of four elements: action, cognition, feelings, and physiology. We are continuously and simultaneously generating a specific activity, a singular thought, an emotion, and concomitant physiology. The time between one behavior and the next is often infinitesimal and immeasurable. The cause of *any* change, immediate or long range, is rooted in the quality world of the person's wants.

After identifying IST statements, the therapeutic goal is to replace them with EST. This is accomplished by asking clients to evaluate their thinking, whether holding fast to IST is helping them. Clearly their self-evaluation is a cognitive function. Moreover, sometimes the most prominent presenting behavior is the cognitive component of total behavior. For these two reasons, reality therapists ask questions such as "Is telling yourself you have no control in your life helping you?" Clients are then encouraged to act *as if* they truly believed that they are in control of their lives and that they can change.

Actions

Therapeutic conversations focus on the component of total behavior over which clients have most direct control. They describe exactly what happened such as what they *did* when they felt anger, jealousy, depression, or resentment. Similarly the reality therapist asks them to describe situations when they chose other actions and how they felt as a result of making more effective choices. Even with seemingly less serious issues, a precise accounting of the use of time can lead to improvement. Losing weight, gaining better control of time, and budgeting more effectively are made easier when keeping a log of exactly what a person eats, how he or she spends each hour of the day, or exactly how much money is spent with every purchase. This laborious assignment focuses the client's perception and cognition on the most controllable part of the total behavior—actions.

Also, with more serious issues such as Axis I or Axis II disorders, the reality therapist applies the principle that reality therapy is a *mental health system* not merely a system for remediating diagnosable mental disorders. The problems are seen as current and are discussed, for the most part, with emphasis on current behavior. However, most of the therapy focuses on the client's mental health even if effective and mentally healthy behaviors are less prominent and less frequent than ineffective adjustment or psychotic behaviors. Though not recommended as a technique now, Glasser in his early reality therapy occasionally asked a patient in a mental hospital, "Would you stop acting crazy so I could talk to you?" Reality therapists perceive clients as partially disturbed and having at least some degree of sanity. In talking to clients about their current mentally healthy behaviors, they ask them to describe their feelings, self-talk, and most emphatically their actions. Even in a mental hospital, a reality therapist talks with clients about what they do when they are not hallucinat-ing, paranoid-ing, schizophrenia-ing, manic-ing, or self-injuring.

Positive symptoms such as assertive and altruistic actions are alternatives and replacements for negative symptoms such as acting out and other harmful choices. In other words the more clients choose positive symptoms, or effective behaviors, the less they generate harmful, violent, or socially unacceptable actions, thinking, and emotions.

The key question under the D of the WDEP system is:

WHAT ARE YOU *DOING*?

This powerful four-word question takes on a degree of complexity and renders reality therapy controversial and even conflictual with other systems of psychotherapy. Each of the words summarizes a guideline useful in understanding and implementing reality therapy.

WHAT implies specificity, being exact and precise. The therapist functions like a television camera, recording specific behaviors with emphasis on actions and observing unique rather than generic or typical actions. While the request "describe a typical day" is helpful, a better question is, "What specifically did you do yesterday?" The therapist helps clients describe what happened within a definite time frame. In family therapy the members describe precisely who said what, how it was said, where the argument took place, and other relevant details. The discussion might include, "When was the last time you spent time together that was enjoyable to all?" The rationale for focusing on actions is clear: Human beings have more direct control over their actions than thoughts or feelings. Paradoxically, people are more aware of their feelings and thoughts, but these elements of total behavior are less easily changed than actions.

ARE implies emphasizing current or recent behaviors, past behaviors as they relate to the present, and past successful in-control choices. Endless discussion of past ineffective behaviors leads clients to unnecessarily highlight their perception of out-of-control behaviors and puts them at a level of undeserved importance. During the first certification week held in Kuwait in 1998, Siddiqa N. M. Hussain stated, "The past is a springboard not a hammock. You don't drown by falling in the water. You drown by staying in it." As with many theories of psychotherapy, reality therapy seems to contain an element of autobiography of its founder William Glasser. The ARE implies focusing on present behaviors. In his biography of Glasser, Roy (2006) states that Glasser was reticent to talk about his early personal life, saying, "Whatever my secret past is, is gonna remain secret" (p. 55). Roy later notes that this emphasis on the present "encapsulated one of the foundation points of Glasser's thinking and might represent his first real break with traditional psychiatry" (p. 87). In describing the connection between healthy interpersonal relationships and current behaviors, Roth and Goldring (2008) state, "Revisiting the painful past can contribute little or nothing to what we need to do now. What we need to do now is improve an important present relationship" (p. 14).

Stressing current behaviors as part of the D (doing) of the WDEP system is more than a mere convenience. Feinauer, Mitchell, Harper, and Dane (1998) found that the adult adjustment of female survivors of abuse was characterized by "hardiness." They described this characteristic as a high level of commitment, control, and challenge. Seen from the perspective of choice theory, it means pursuing wants and achieving a sense of power and achievement with emphasis on *current* wants and needs.

YOU implies emphasizing clients' controllable behaviors rather than the uncontrollable behaviors of other people. Clients victimized by circumstances, by history, or by other people often wish to discuss behaviors that are out of control. The skillful practice of reality therapy means gently leading clients to discuss their choices, their possibilities, their hopes, and their goals.

DOING implies discussing all aspects of total behavior: action, thinking, feeling, and physiology, with emphasis on the first and most controllable component.

An accumulation of therapy interventions focusing on "What are you doing?" can precede or follow a discussion of "What direction are you taking in your life?" "Where are you headed?" "If you continue to do what you're doing, where will your current system of choices—your suitcase of behavior—take you?" "Are you headed in a desirable direction?" This final question contains the seeds of self-evaluation.

EXPLORING EVALUATION

The key questions under the E of the WDEP system are:
IS WHAT YOU'RE DOING *HELPING* YOU?
IS WHAT YOU WANT *ATTAINABLE?*

The foundation for practicing reality therapy is establishing a safe environment in which clients freely and spontaneously self-disclose. Incorporating the principles of empathy, reality therapists attempt to see the world as the clients see it as well as how clients see themselves in relation to the world around them. Skilled reality therapists take a step further in that they see clients not as objects acted upon by their external worlds but as agents capable of improved life directions and more effective choices. Most importantly, they see clients as *current* choice makers.

Having assisted clients to clarify, define, and express their current wants and needs—both fulfilled and unmet—as well as their present behaviors, reality therapists help clients conduct a fearless and searching self-evaluation. This task, like the entire practice of reality therapy, is deceptively simple. Glasser (2005b) describes self-evaluation as the core of reality therapy. The process of self-evaluation, the most typically representative set of interventions for reality therapy, is a *sine qua non*, a necessary precondition for behavioral change. Wubbolding (1990, 1991, 2008a, 2008c) describes self-evaluation as a keystone in the arch of procedures. Remove the keystone and the arch crumbles and becomes rubble.

Self-evaluation is not a creation of choice theory or reality therapy. George Washington stated, "Every person is the best judge of what relates to his own interests or concerns . . . errors once discovered are more than half amended." Implying that self-evaluation works better than the exclusive use of external evaluation, Abraham Lincoln once remarked, "You don't improve a soldier by shooting him" (Wubbolding, 2009a, p. 20). Much has been written about self-evaluation in the context of reality therapy. In applying reality therapy to management, Pierce (2007) states, "Every worker brings to his job a special genius that can only be uncovered when the worker feels trusted to self-evaluate and continuously improve" (p. 50). In describing classroom intervention strategies for teachers, Hoglund (2007) stresses asking students such questions as "Are you following the rules?" "Is what you're doing against the rules?" (p. 51). Richardson (2001) applies the principles of reality therapy to youth who present a challenge to adults through their antisocial behavior. He states that such individuals are accustomed to having others evaluate their behavior and have not learned the crucial life skill of self-evaluation. In his lectures Glasser frequently describes happy people as spending their lives evaluating their own behavior and unhappy people as evaluating the behavior of others.

When discussing the central place of self-evaluation in choice theory and in the practice of reality therapy, Wubbolding (1998) emphasizes that questions focusing on self-evaluation need to be explicit and precise. Therapists cannot assume that people voluntarily seeking help have evaluated their behavior and wants. Many people desire an outcome but do not see that their behavior is ineffective. They have not connected their quality world with their total behavior (see Figure 4.1). Change only occurs after people decide that their behavior is not working for them, that their wants are unattainable, and that they can control their own behavior, not that of others.

Effective self-evaluation rests on the inner assessment made by clients and on relevant and targeted questions asked by the therapist. Through this interactional process, clients make specific judgments about their total behavior, quality world, and other components in their choice systems.

Types of Self-Evaluation

Self-evaluation constitutes the core of reality therapy. It is the keystone in the arch of reality therapy interventions. From the perspective of reality therapy, clients change behavior *only* after evaluating that something in their behavioral system, their world of wants, or their range of perceptions is unsatisfactory to themselves or others. Wubbolding, Brickell, Loi, and Al-Rashidi (2001) examined 22 types of self-evaluation. They state, "Self-evaluation is a tool for helping people choose more effectively. Change for the better is built on the inner judgment that there is a better available life path" (p. 36). They add that the skillful reality therapist works in a fluid and flexible manner and generates a wide variety of pertinent questions geared to each situation. These questions help clients examine each component of the choice theory system: quality world, total behavior, and perceptual system.

1. *Overall behavioral direction and purpose.* "Is the overall direction of your life taking you closer or farther away from your goal?" "Is it bringing you closer or farther away from the important people in your life?"
2. *Choices.* "Do you believe you can control your choices?" "Do you believe you can control the choices of others (e.g., children, spouse, partner, employees, manager)?" "What choices have you made that have been especially helpful to you? Unhelpful to you or to others?"
3. *Specific behaviors: effective or ineffective.* "Are your current specific behaviors helping you or hurting you?" "What are you doing that is keeping you worse off than you want to be?" "Are your specific behaviors connecting you or disconnecting you from the people around you?"

4. *Specific actions related to rules.* "Are your current actions against a rule or policy of the organization?" "What are the laws that touch on your actions and do any of your actions violate a law?" "Will your current actions keep you free of trouble?"

5. *Specific actions: acceptable or unacceptable.* "Do your current actions seem reasonable or unreasonable to the people around you?" "Is what you're doing against any unwritten rule?"

6. *Thinking behaviors: ineffective or effective self-talk.* "How do such statements as, 'I can't change' or 'they won't let me' or 'I'm going to keep doing what is harmful to me' impact your effort to change your behavior?" "How does this type of self-talk undermine your actions?" "How does it impact the people around you?" "If you continue to think pessimistically (or optimistically), will you get closer or farther away from the people around you?"

7. *Belief system.* "How does what you believe about human nature add to or subtract from your life?" "Does your belief about family roles impede or enhance harmony in your family?"

8. *Feeling behaviors: helpful or harmful emotions.* "Do your positive and negative feelings attract people or put them off?" "What effect does your anger, resentment, patience, tolerance have on your physiology/health?"

9. *Clients' best interests: specific actions and thoughts that enhance or diminish their long-term interest.* "How does the short-term gain of your choice strengthen or diminish the long-term gain for you?" "Does driving people away from you (or attracting them to you) strengthen or weaken you?" "What effect does this process have on your long-term interests?"

10. *High-quality or low-quality behavior. Quality is the standard.* "What effect does your behavior have on the quality of your work, of your relationships?" "How does your contribution add to the quality of the organization, of the classroom, of the family?"

11. *Life enhancement.* Life is sometimes improved even though a specific action might not be immediately satisfying. "Do your current life goals or action choices enhance or diminish your overall lifestyle?"

12. *Behavior as measured by goals of the organization.* Because all human beings live and work in organizations, it is often helpful to ask about the congruence between their personal aims and those of the organization. "Does what you want from your job match what the institution is attempting to achieve?"

13. *Wants: realistic or attainable.* This form of self-evaluation occupies a central place in therapy with involuntary clients. When the client desires a clearly unattainable goal, the reality therapist can ask, "Is there a reasonable possibility of getting what you want in the near or distant future?"

14. *Wants: beneficial or harmful to self, others or the organization.* At first glance, all wants in the quality world appear desirable. However, a reality therapist helps clients examine the benefits of achieving their wants. "Are your wants truly in your best interest on a short-term and a long-term basis?"

15. *Wants: precise and clearly enough defined so as to cause consistent action.* "If you had a clear idea of what you want, what would you be doing differently or better than what you're doing now?"

16. *Wants as nonnegotiable, highly desirable, or mere wishes.* "Which of your wants would you describe as 'can't live without,' and which would you describe as 'it would be nice if I had what I want'?" "Which is most important and which is least important?"

17. *Perceptions: viewpoint plus or minus.* "When you compare your inner sense of your limitations with the external ways in which you think others perceive you, are you being fair to yourself?" "How will it be helpful to you if you see the glass as half full . . . half empty?"

18. *Perceptions: locus of control.* "Given your strengths and limitations, what do you have control over and what do you not have control over?" "Whose behavior can you control?" "How much of all your trouble or success are you causing?"

19. *Values and behavior: congruence or lack of it.* "You've described what you hold as values and principles and what you think is important. How important is it to you that your actions fit these values?"

"Under what circumstances is it acceptable for you to violate your values?"

20. *Level of commitment: firm enough to achieve desired outcomes.* "Will your current level of commitment get the job done?" "If you say 'I'll try,' is that enough to accomplish your goal?"

21. *Evaluation of the plan of action.* "If you follow through on your plan, how will your life be better?" "If you don't follow through on your plan, what will happen?" "Is your plan simple, attainable, measurable, immediate, and controlled by you, and are you committed to carrying out your plan?"

22. *Professional self-evaluation.* This procedure, the keystone in the practice of reality therapy, also applies to the behavior of the therapist. Supervisors who use reality therapy ask their interns to self-evaluate by asking themselves such questions as: "How am I facilitating my own personal and professional growth?" "Is the quality of my service to the public and to my employer at a level acceptable to me and to the institution employing me?" "How can I increase the quality of my service?"

The clinical experience of reality therapists seems to verify the axiom described by Wubbolding (1998): "As human beings we have inside of us a characteristic that I have called *an undying belief in behaviors that do not work*" (p. 196). If something isn't working, do more of it. For example, if shouting at children doesn't get the desired result, shout louder and more often. How many people have experienced misplacing car keys, glasses, or important papers? Persistent and repeated searching often yields no results. The reason for repeating ineffective behaviors is that the person does not see an immediately available alternative choice. A more effective behavior entails extracting an alternative choice from the behavioral suitcase or driving the behavioral car in a different direction. It is far more helpful to sit still for a moment and ask, "Is this really helpful?" If the answer is "no," an alternative choice is possible and the ineffective behavior can be abandoned as the search for a better choice begins.

Self-Evaluation as Judgment

Self-evaluation is more than a mere description of behavior. The heart of this procedure lies in an internal *judgment* facilitated by the therapist. Consequently, clients restructure their thinking, which is a necessary prerequisite for more need-satisfying behavioral changes. This contemplation is more than temporary idle musing; it is an ongoing process learned by clients and practiced until it becomes habitual. Similar to rowing a canoe upstream, the art of self-evaluation requires a commitment to repeatedly assess one's own effective choices lest old behaviors reappear. Many clients express this process with words similar to, "This is difficult, but I'm in it for the long haul." Helping clients self-evaluate may be as straightforward as asking them whether a behavior is helpful or hurtful, satisfying or unsatisfying, efficacious or futile. However, this procedure is deceptively simple. People learning reality therapy frequently skip this central and all important procedure by too rapidly moving from, "What are you doing?" to "What's your plan?"

The D (doing) and the E (self-evaluation) are a mirror held before clients with questions, "Tell me what you're doing and whether it is working for you; tell me what you want and is obtaining it to your advantage?" or "If you do nothing differently, will anything in your life change?" This last incisive question serves as an effective tool for working with clients feeling powerless and hopeless. It presumes that they have the strength within them to choose more wisely. Clearly, reality therapy rests on a positive belief in human nature and the conviction that, if shown the way, clients can discover choices they had never previously identified or dreamed could be made available to them.

Levels of Self-Evaluation

Self-evaluation is a chosen thinking behavior whose purpose is to reflect on every element of the choice theory system. And yet it is more than a reflection, more than a musing, more than an observation. It is a judgment. And like all judgments, it is made with varying levels of insight. Some people seem to have very little insight and evaluate their behaviors as helpful when an outside observer can clearly judge the ineffectiveness and destructiveness of the other person's behaviors. For instance, in spite of surveillance cameras, many bank robbers wear no disguise, fail to research a proper getaway, and even lack an effective plan for concealing the loot. Because of these would-be robbers' inability to self-evaluate, the FBI has advised them to find another line of work. Individuals abusing drugs evaluate their behavior and conclude that drugs are good for them. A student procrastinates studying for exams or doing assignments as a result of inadequate self-evaluation.

Individuals do not self-evaluate in a vacuum. Information serves as a foundation for effective want and need satisfaction. Consequently, there are levels of insight and judgment that aid in a person's self-evaluation.

Level I: Self-Evaluation With Little or No Information

The founders of the United States knew that self-evaluation without information provided by others would lead to self-destruction. If each branch of government stood without checks and balances, the American system would have quickly failed after the American Revolution. Awarding a psychology license to a person self-evaluating "I am a competent psychologist" without co-verification would be an outlandish policy. Many high school driver education instructors encounter 16-year-old students who believe they are expert drivers and then discover that those students require information about how to start and stop the car.

Every marriage therapist has encountered a spouse who sincerely believes that he or she is patient, kind, compassionate, thrifty, and loving toward the children and that his or her partner is demanding, impatient, and intolerant. When talking to the second spouse, the therapist discovers that there are two sides to this story. Experienced therapists help clients become more circumspect in their self-evaluations. They help them see their behavior in a new light and from a new perspective. It is not unknown for people to have not 30 years of experience but one year repeated 30 times. Therapists' questions focusing on self-evaluation aim at helping clients make each year better than the previous one.

Level II: Self-Evaluation With Knowledge and Information

When people deepen their level of information and knowledge about their own behavior or the attainability of their wants, they achieve a more cultivated level of self-evaluation. Taking a psychology course leads to a judgment about the vast body of knowledge required for a license. After learning the intricacies of driving an automobile, the 16-year-old student is in a better position to self-evaluate. When a spouse details the other person's behavior—miserly not thrifty, impatient not patient, unsympathetic not compassionate—the result is information previously unknown. The person receiving the information can weigh its value and relevance. Information alone does not ensure change, but a willingness to view change as useful can lead to better human relationships, the preeminent goal of the practice of reality therapy.

Level III: Self-Evaluation Based on Feedback and a Standard

Information, feedback, and standards provide the basis for the highest level of self-evaluation. The student of psychology passes an exam required by law. The driver education instructor presents "corrective feedback" to students to help them to move to a higher skill level and verifies that the skill achieved suffices for the student to pass or at least take the driver's test. In marriage therapy the reality therapist assists spouses to present feedback in ways acceptable to their partners and to help the partners receive it, evaluate it, and, if useful, act on it.

Self-evaluation is part of the developmental process of mental health. It is a pathway from the negative and ineffective behaviors characterized by "I give up," negative symptoms, and addictions to the effective behaviors of "I'll do it," positive symptoms, and positive addictions (see Figure 4.1). A person driving a car and mistakenly believing that he is headed in his desired direction continues onward until he comes to the realization that "I'm lost" or "my current direction is not getting me where I want to go." The self-evaluation "What I'm doing is not working" is a prerequisite for change. Skilled reality therapists have in their suitcase of behavior a range of questions that help clients evaluate their behavior and make judgments about it that serve as a foundation for action planning.

Self-Evaluation: Case Examples

The following examples illustrate an application of the principle of self-evaluation to clients.

Lou, 17, is referred to a therapist because of his acting-out behaviors. He is flunking in school and often truant and has been arrested for the occasional use of illegal substances. The therapist helps him define several wants: to be left alone, to be off probation, and to live with his father instead of with his mother. The reality therapist assists him to describe in detail his current behaviors as well as how the adults in his environment lecture him, punish him, and endlessly threaten him. The therapist asks him to evaluate the realistic attainability of his wants, the effectiveness of his actions in fulfilling his wants, and his self-talk, "Nobody is going to tell me what to do." If Lou decides that his current actions and thinking are ineffective and are leading him in a destructive direction, the therapist helps him make alternative plans.

Shelby, 38, worked for a building contractor, has been laid off, has given up looking for work, and spends 6–7 hours per day watching television or surfing the web. His wife coerces him to see a reality therapist and adds that he is drinking excessively. The reality therapist empathizes with Shelby's feelings of depression and powerlessness and asks him such questions as, "What kind of behaviors do you have available to you that will help you feel better? Looking for work is the most obvious, but there are other choices that can give you at least temporary relief." Sometimes the best way to address powerlessness is to help clients more effectively fulfill their need for belonging. The reality therapist might help Shelby and his wife evaluate their time spent together and plan activities requiring high levels of energy that are productive and are performed without arguing, blaming, and criticizing.

The work of the reality therapist with Lou and Shelby described above is a snapshot of how self-evaluation applies. There are many more ways to apply the WDEP system to these cases.

Indirect Self-Evaluation

Straightforward direct questioning is the most prevalent form of self-evaluation. However, a subtler example of self-evaluation helps clients externalize a problem and see it from a different perspective. A technique borrowed from Erickson and his followers consists of the use of metaphors, narratives, or stories. For instance, an anecdote beginning with "Your situation reminds me of someone I heard about who was faced with a similar challenge," followed by a description of a comparable problem happily resolved, helps the client gain a sense of hope in that others have made effective and helpful choices. It also allows the client to look at his or her own behavior and view it as helping or impeding progress. Wubbolding (1991) describes metaphors that can be applied to self-evaluation: repeatedly looking for lost car keys in the same place, spinning the wheels of a car, incessant yelling at the kids, the myth of Sisyphus condemned to forever push a rock up a hill only to have it roll down and have to be pushed up again. These and many other metaphors can be integrated into the self-evaluation component of the WDEP system.

Sufficiency of Self-Evaluation

The question is frequently asked: "Is self-evaluation sufficient? What is the role of the client's external or outer world? How does it impinge on the client's judgment?" In a perfect world or if human beings existed in their preternatural state of innocence with an untrammeled tendency to choose only the good, the true, and the beautiful, each person's self-evaluation could stand alone without boundaries or information provided by others.

Genuine behavioral change occurs subsequent to the inner judgment or self-evaluation conducted by clients. However, such judgments do not exist separate from the standards of family, employers, organizations, and society. Hence, the quality of the individual's self-evaluation depends not only on his or her own internal standards but also upon the expectations and standards of others. Asking clients to evaluate their behavior against their internal standard of what they want is a beginning but is not always definitive or decisive. Families, employers, and organizations establish standards of quality. An employee of an automobile company is expected to possess skills necessary for meeting job specifications. These specifications might differ from those for a similar job in another company. Parents from diverse cultures set a wide range of standards of behavior for their children. In helping clients evaluate their own behavior, reality therapists use standards of systems established by others in the clients' various milieux.

Wubbolding (2000a) states,

> The three levels of self-evaluation demonstrate a developmental process based on levels of knowledge. . . . Enlightened self-evaluation transcends a whimsical, uninformed and naïve feeling of quality. It

includes informational input and feedback from peers or mentors in the context of standards of performance. . . . Clients students, employees and professional people function more efficiently when they conduct on-going, fearless and searching self-assessments of their lives and then decide how to add genuine quality to them. (p. 150)

PLANNING FOR CHANGE

The key question under the P of the WDEP system is:
WHAT IS YOUR *PLAN?*

Enhancing mental health or moving from ineffective symptoms to effective symptoms (Figure 4.2) happens when clients decide to improve their lives and then make plans for satisfying their wants and needs. The reality therapist facilitates plan making and instructs clients on the characteristics of successful planning: $SAMI^2C^3$.

- Simple, not overly complicated, easy to understand, geared to client's developmental level.
- Attainable, not grandiose or out of reach. The client sees it as realistic and feasible.
- Measurable, not vague or abstract. The client can answer the question, "When will you do it?"
- Immediate, not unnecessarily delayed. The client sometimes rehearses the plan during the therapy session.
- Involved. The therapist does not leave the client on his or her own and can be involved in the plan as appropriate.
- Controlled by the planner, not dependent on others' behavior. The client regulates execution of the plan.
- Committed to, not characterized by, "I'll try" or "Probably." Plan is firm and fixed.
- Consistent or repetitive, not whimsically or occasionally carried out. The most effective plan is repeated often until it is habitual.

Clients themselves initiate the most efficacious plans with the help of reality therapists eliciting SAMIC plans through skillful but simple questioning. Some clients, especially in the early stages of counseling, are unable or reluctant to originate their own plans. Therefore, a second level of planning is needed—that is, plans jointly formulated by therapist and client.

When the therapeutic alliance is strong, reality therapists feel free to suggest specific tactical plans. They are less forthcoming with suggestions about strategic planning or the overall life direction of clients. Plans initiated by the helper are most effective when clients have clearly indicated their desire to change and have evaluated their behavior—more specifically that prior actions have not helped them. Wubbolding (2000a) states, "The mistake made by neophyte, and even at times experienced practitioners of reality therapy, is to impose a plan too quickly on an unwilling or resistant person or to indulge in paternalistic (or maternalistic) advice giving" (p.151).

The language of planning includes tactful and careful wording of questions based on the perceived receptivity and readiness of the client. A hasty rush to action planning can result in client resistance. The gentle phrasing of questions such as, "could you" is often acceptable to clients. With appropriate timing, reality therapists follow this question with "would you" and "will you?"

APPLICABILITY OF THE WDEP SYSTEM OF REALITY THERAPY

Reality therapy claims a moderately widespread body of empirical research, demonstrating its effectiveness with clients who present with many psychological issues. It has been *applied* on a more far-reaching basis to children, adolescents, and adults (W. Glasser, 2000a; N. Glasser, 1980, 1989). The use of the procedures is limited only by the skill and creativity of the practitioner. From the perspective of reality therapy, human behaviors are not static conditions. They are classified as a series of choices—both effective and ineffective, helpful or harmful, productive or destructive, enhancing or diminishing mental health. Even psychotic individuals retain some measure of constructive ability to choose. Despite their pathology, the contents of their behavioral suitcases do not completely exclude the ability to choose positive behaviors at least occasionally. Reality therapists attempt to help clients build on their "sane" behaviors expanding and enlarging their successes. Consequently, whether the behavior constitutes an adjustment issue, antisocial behavior, negative addiction, or psychosis, reality therapists, while not ignoring problem behavior, spend most of their therapeutic conversation discussing alternatives to the presenting problem.

Reality therapy as a system has not only been applied to mental health issues. It has been expanded to include applications to relationships (Ford, 1979), education (Greene, 1994; Gilchrist Banks, 2009; Parish & Parish, 1999; Sullo, 2007), spirituality (Roy, 2005), parenting (Buck, 2000; Primason, 2004), recovery from child abuse (Ellsworth, 2007), criminal justice (Myers & Jackson, 2002; Pierce & Taylor, 2008), and self-help (Britzman, 2009).

THE LANGUAGE OF CHOICE THEORY AND REALITY THERAPY

Regardless of cultural differences, all human beings communicate with words. This principle in no way contradicts the fact that much communication is nonverbal. Nevertheless, words occupy a central place in all human interaction, especially in psychotherapy. The language of choice theory and reality therapy reflects an attempt to bring mental health processes to the public while using understandable language.

Language of Inner Control

Winston Churchill once remarked that words are the only things that last forever. Though it would be presumptuous to assume that clients are profoundly impacted by every word used by a psychotherapist, still language reflecting positive regard facilitates clients' self-disclosure. Additionally, the language of inner control communicates a message to clients that they have more control over their behavior than originally thought. When clients learn to use phrases such as, "I chose to do it" rather than "He *made* me do it" or when they replace "You *make* me angry" with "I'm anger-ing," they learn that they can empower themselves to regulate their lives more effectively. In speaking of the harmfulness of external control language and the underlying rationale for its replacement, Glasser and Glasser (1999) theorize:

> External control language always harms and often destroys the relationship we must have for happiness and success. External control is a plague on all humanity.
>
> Choice theory (and reality therapy) is exactly the opposite. Its language, never bossy or controlling, is always an attempt to work out the differences between people in a way that satisfies both parties. For example, open, fair and non-coercive negotiation is always the choice of people who use this theory. They will listen, support, sustain, tolerate and be patient with one another.
>
> The difference between the two languages is startling. External control speech is peppered with the imperative tense, with *should*, *must* and *have to*, plus threats of punishment if you don't do what you're told and promises of reward if you do. Choice theory (and reality therapy) language helps us to work out problems with one another; external control language increases them. (pp. vii–viii)

In their highly useful manual for implementing the language of internal control, the authors apply communication skills to parenting, love, and marriage, teacher and student, manager and employee. They caution,

> It takes time to learn to use a new language that is different from what has been used on you all your life and that you began using when you were very young. . . . You will find that most are intrigued. It is not that people are against using choice theory, it is that most of them don't even know it exists. (p. 107)

Clear and Uncomplicated Language

The principles of choice theory and reality therapy have been extended and significantly developed since the founding of reality therapy by William Glasser in 1965. From the very beginning, the ideas have been clearly enunciated and the vocabulary easily understood. Glasser and Wubbolding (1995) stated:

In formulating and extending the principles of reality therapy Wubbolding and Glasser have made a conscious decision to use easily understood words. The use of simple words, such as *belonging, power, fun, freedom, choices, wants,* and *plans,* is not an accident. The happy result of this effort has been to introduce basic concepts of mental health to new audiences. Yet this demystification and relative understandability of the concepts is a two-edged sword, and the principles of reality therapy are more difficult to practice than to understand. (p. 302)

Glasser and Wubbolding suggest that developing a language peculiar to the theory and practice of reality therapy would be an easy but seductive pathway. Such formulations would serve only to mystify and to erect barriers that render mental health less accessible to those in most need of it. Most emphatically, Glasser (2005a) presents mental health as a *public* issue. From the very beginning, his effort has been to teach that human beings make choices and are responsible for them (Glasser, 1960, 1965). For many, this has been a source of hope, adding to self-confidence, self-worth, a sense of enhanced inner control, and better human relationships.

The relative absence of esoteric language might lead a learner to conclude that the practice of reality therapy is simplistic and superficial. Some have erroneously viewed reality therapy as a mere problem-solving technique with too much emphasis on personal choice and too little emphasis on the impact of external forces. The easily understood language can facilitate both client empowerment and evoke erroneous perceptions about the ease of gaining self-regulation. However, certification in reality therapy through The William Glasser Institute, formerly known as the Institute for Reality Therapy, requires 18 months for its completion and consists of training workshops and practica. Wubbolding (2000a) states, "To see the world through the lenses of choice theory and reality therapy requires time, effort and the unlearning of previously learned skills which often interfere with the effective use of reality therapy" (p. 165).

The language describing choice theory and reality therapy, while remaining easily understood, has undergone gradual but continuous change. The reason lies in the extensions, refinements, and developments of the theory itself. It existed in a seminal way at the Ventura School for

Girls in the early 1960s. The Eight Steps (Glasser, 1972) summarizing reality therapy preceded the most up-to-date description, the WDEP system. In 1996 Glasser changed *control theory* to *choice theory* to further emphasize the internal origin of human behavior.

The minimal use of technical language explains the popularity of reality therapy and paradoxically the inattention it has received in the professional world. Many people not trained in psychology, counseling, social work, or psychiatry find reality therapy a sensible way to look at human nature. Yet until recently, some professionals have not seen the depth and intricacies of choice theory or the many proven applications of reality therapy. Furthermore the ever-increasing body of research has helped to increase the credibility of choice theory and reality therapy.

Others have stated that reality therapy underemphasizes environmental and social influences. For instance, Murdock (2004) states,

> Reality therapy is often faulted for ignoring social influences on behavior. Reality therapy does not seem to take these phenomena into account. Glasser would probably say that going along with the crowd is more a result of a failure to wake up and make choices than to any magical power of social forces. (p. 273)

In fact, reality therapy emphasizes the controllable aspects of human life. Making plans to change external circumstances, increase social justice, or alter unfair rules are quite congruent with the practice of reality therapy and public mental health.

ASKING QUESTIONS IN THERAPY

Freud proposed that the royal road to the unconscious was dream interpretation (Luborsky, O'Reilly-Landry, & Arlow, 2008). Choice theory and reality therapy identify their own royal road—the road to internal control. The most direct pathway used by reality therapists is skillful questioning related to the five human needs, the quality world, total behavior, and perceptions that are operationalized in the WDEP system. Relevant questions assist clients in gaining insights, seeing relationships, and arriving at plans and solutions. The use of questions serves four purposes:

1. *Entering the world of the clients.* Exploring with clients what they want from family, friends, job, colleagues, themselves, and therapist communicates respect and helps the therapist become part of clients' quality worlds. Appropriately timed questions address a prerequisite for therapeutic progress. They establish, maintain, and strengthen the therapeutic alliance. They enhance empathy and positive regard but avoid the trap of endless reflection on debilitating feelings. To the client stating "I'm depressed," the question "Would you like to feel better?" replaces the classical statement "You're feeling powerless today."

2. *Gathering information.* Many questions often characterize intake interviews. When the therapeutic relationship develops, the reality therapist takes questions to a different level. Gathering information about how clients spend their time precedes further questions focusing on self-evaluation. Insights helpful to clients can be gained by asking what others want from them, how others see their behavior, or what boundaries others are imposing on the clients. A reality therapist often asks a depressed (depress-ing) person, "How did you spend your time yesterday?" and "Did watching TV for 6 hours help you relinquish your feelings of being down in the dumps?" However, gathering information is not the ultimate goal of questioning. It is a prerequisite for achieving the more important purposes listed below.

3. *Giving information.* Clients gain valuable information often not explicitly foreseen by the therapist when asking questions. Inquiring "What did you do yesterday to satisfy your need for belonging? What did you do to connect with even one person in a way that helped you to lessen your pain?" communicates a powerful lesson by sending a message: "*You have choices available to you. Your life can improve. Your upsetness will not last forever. You have more control than you think you have.*" Clients often receive this information and filter it through the relationship filter and the valuing filter (see Figure 4.1). They see the connection between their feelings and actions. They learn that what they want is connected to their total behavior and that they have more choices than previously believed, resulting in a sense of hope for a better future.

4. *Helping clients take more effective control and choose more wisely.*
   Through precise questioning, reality therapists assist clients to
   identify their motivations—that is, their needs for love or belonging, power or inner control, freedom or independence, and fun or
   enjoyment. Clients learn to focus their perceptions on their actions
   rather than on feelings that might slow down or obstruct progress.
   This level of questioning leads clients to evaluate the attainability of
   their wants, the efficacy of their actions, and the helpfulness of their
   self-talk, all of which are prerequisites for action planning.

Persons extremely receptive to changing their lives might be willing to
listen to lecturing from people wiser than themselves as well as advice and
cogent arguments given by more experienced individuals. But for clients
lacking such a predisposition, reality therapists assist them to *look in a mirror* by observing their own behavior and evaluating it through the use of
the D and the E of the WDEP system. Artistic and targeted questioning by
the therapist facilitates this process by helping clients define wants related
to their needs and formulate SAMIC plans. The principle of the "buffalo
bridle" (Weinberg, 1985) applies: "You can get a buffalo to do whatever
you want it to do . . . if it wants to do it."

In summary, reality therapy embraces as paramount the importance of
the therapist's skill in establishing a trusting relationship. The client must
see the therapist as a skilled, knowledgeable, and helpful ally. The WDEP
system, with its emphasis on client self-evaluation, provides an array of
skills that mental health workers can implement. These skills are expressed
not only with empathic listening but also with well-timed and persistent
questions eliciting clearly defined wants, precisely described behaviors
(total), forthright self-evaluations, and achievable plans. A major question
remains: Does reality therapy work? Is it effective? Is there any group or
types of behaviors with which it is ineffective?

5

Evaluation

This chapter provides a sampling of research studies supporting reality therapy with special emphasis on cultural issues. These studies and adaptations indicate the universal applicability of choice theory and its delivery system reality therapy. Wubbolding and Brickell (2000) emphasize that reality therapy has been studied in a variety of settings, including mental health, education, substance abuse, and corrections, and in various cultures. Therefore, a workable description of "culture" provides an appropriate base for discussion.

Webster's Concise Desk Encyclopedia (1995) defines *culture* as "the way of life of a particular society or group of people, including patterns of thought, belief, behavior, customs, traditions, rituals, dress, and language, as well as art, music and literature" (p. 160). In an increasingly globalized and multicultural world society with access to instant communication, writers and therapists are making an intense effort to adapt counseling and psychotherapy theories to diverse populations. Frew and Spiegler (2008) state,

> This is an exciting and challenging time to be entering the profession because there is an important shift taking place in the theory and practice of contemporary psychotherapies. The demographic

patterns in the United States are changing rapidly, and those changes are reflected in the clients who are seeking help for their psychological problems. (p. 1)

Moreover, professional psychotherapy, and especially reality therapy, is accepted in cultures around the world.

CULTURAL ISSUES

A major concern in the helping professions is the mental health of minorities and providing services for the "culturally different" (i.e., non-White people). Negy (2008) states that many writers on multiculturalism assert that because counseling and psychotherapy theories have been developed in Western Europe and in North America, they are ineffective and not applicable to the culturally different. He cites Sue and Sue (2003), "Effective multicultural therapy means using modalities and defining goals that are consistent with their racial, cultural, ethnic, gender and sexual orientation backgrounds" (p. 17). However, Negy adds, "All considered, currently, the assertion that psychological principles and therapeutic techniques apply to Whites but may not apply to non-Whites appears to be unsubstantiated" (p. 14). He emphasizes the relevance of the psychology profession when therapists take into consideration the ethnic background of their clients. Consequently, it is the responsibility of therapists to be as knowledgeable as possible about the cultural values of their clients. The "Guidelines on Multicultural Education, Training, Research, Practice, and Organizational Change for Psychologists" (American Psychological Association, 2002b) state, "Psychologists are encouraged to recognize the importance of multicultural sensitivity/responsiveness, knowledge, and understanding about ethnicity and racially different individuals" (Guideline 2). Guideline 5 states, "Psychologists strive to apply culturally-appropriate skills in clinical and other applied psychological practices."

North American Minority Groups

The increasing number of minority groups in North America and their need for mental health services have prompted professional groups to heighten their awareness and skills for providing services for individuals and groups with a wide range of behaviors and values as well as world-views quite different from those of many therapists. Reality therapy is an eminently useful tool in that the techniques can be adapted to virtually any client. Its underlying theory, choice theory, is an explanation of human nature, including motivation, behavior, and perceptions. It is universal and therefore not culturally encapsulated. Applications to specific groups include but are not limited to the examples below.

African Americans

In working with African Americans, Fajors and Negy (2008) suggest that because successful therapy requires a trusting therapeutic alliance, the issue of race should be a topic for discussion in the beginning of therapy. For some clients racial differences might present a barrier that can be dealt with by discussing whether racial differences present an issue. The authors remind practitioners that African Americans often bring to counseling conventional issues such as marriage, parent–child relationships, and self-esteem concerns. Of special importance is the commitment to the church. Fajors and Negy state, "Among African Americans commitment to religion and church involvement have been found to correlate with improved family relationships, less marital conflict, and better adjustment among adolescents" (p. 171). They add that elderly African Americans live longer if they are involved with their churches. From the choice theory point of view, it is evident that spirituality and worship with all their implications are part of their quality worlds and need satisfying. Such involvement appears to satisfy the generic needs for belonging, power or inner control, freedom, and fun or enjoyment. From the perspective of the WDEP (wants, doing, evaluation, and planning) system of reality therapy, while respecting individual differences, therapists can help clients clarify their spiritual wants and even encourage them to be connected to their churches.

Wilson and Stith (1991) provide several principles useful for counseling African Americans: *social support systems*, which provide strength to individuals; *differences in values,* such as emphasis on sharing, spirituality, and respect for elders; and *overcoming communication barriers*, which might result from clients' hesitation to speak to a counselor because they don't speak as the counselor speaks. The resulting silence might be misinterpreted as resistance and lack of cooperation. Corey (2009) adds that helpers need to pass a test for their sincerity and genuineness. The effective reality therapist asks clients about what they want from the world around them, how they feel connected with family and community, how they perceive the world differently from the people in their environment, and how they deal with barriers to their need satisfaction. This effort aims at enhancing the therapeutic relationship and passing the test of sincerity and genuineness.

It would seem from the research of Okonji (1995) that reality therapy fulfills the above prerequisites. In studying African American male students in a Job Corps setting, Okonji compared reality therapy and person-centered therapy and found they preferred reality therapy to a statistically significant degree. Okonji, Ososkie, and Pullos (1996) confirmed the necessity of counseling minority ethnic groups with reality therapy and other directive approaches. They conclude, "If agencies or counseling programs need to train people to serve ethnic minority clients, they need to consider various treatment modalities, especially directive approaches such as reality therapy" (p. 337).

Puerto Ricans

Morales (1995) stated that reality therapy is an exceptionally workable and effective model to use with Puerto Ricans. The theory and practice of reality therapy can be appropriately applied to Puerto Rican culture described by Morales as including characteristics such as *responsibility to others*—especially in the family with resulting guilt when obligations are not fulfilled; *expectation that problems will be solved quickly*—because, as Morales states, "Our accomplishments as a people consists in obtaining results as soon as possible" (p. 13); *identification with the disadvantaged*—as exemplified in gratitude leading to altruism, which leads people to connect with each other in a common cause; and *conservativism in decision making*—as demonstrated in the hesitation to take risks, expressed in the commonly used phrase, "It is better to have (a current) known evil than an evil to be known (in the future)." Morales attributes much collective progress and stability in the social structure to a deliberative decision-making process. A final characteristic is *loyalty and hospitality*; many times, self-interests are secondary to the needs of others.

Although controlled studies focusing on the effectiveness of specific theories for Puerto Ricans are few in number, Arbona and Virella (2008) suggest that "short term behavioral and cognitive behavioral group interventions, as well as individual cognitive behavioral and interpersonal psychotherapy lead to positive outcomes with Puerto Ricans in the U.S. and on the island" (p. 120). They point to the therapeutic alliance as the foundation for successful therapy.

Skillful reality therapists using the WDEP system as a brief therapy help Puerto Rican clients build on their quality world wants that include close relationships with others. They also realize that self-evaluation, a cognitive process, is not an impulsive process and that the decision to alter one's life even in small ways—that is, to formulate action plans—cannot be rushed but is a reflective and thoughtful process.

Characteristics of Reality Therapy Relevant to Cultural Diversity

Reality therapy contains inherent qualities making it applicable to minorities in America: African Americans, Hispanics, women, gay men and lesbians, persons of Middle Eastern descent, Asians, Native Americans, First Nation, Pacific Islanders, and many others.

- *Brevity.* Clients often wish to see quick results. While reality therapy offers no magical solutions, it can be used to help clients gain a sense of inner control within a short time frame. Once mistakenly criticized as a superficial problem-solving method, it has achieved more prominence with the arrival of managed care.
- *Respect for client.* When applying the WDEP system of reality therapy appropriately, the reality therapist demonstrates respect by assisting clients to define, clarify, and achieve what they want. Asking clients what they want from therapy, from their environment, and from themselves shows that the therapist regards them as valued individuals.
- *Inner control.* Some members of minority groups feel discriminated against, denied opportunities, and disengaged from the larger society. Because reality therapy is based on an internal control theory emphasizing choices, it is possible to conclude that reality therapists engage

in "blaming the victim." Nothing could be further from the truth. The accurate implementation of the principles of reality therapy focuses on empowering clients. By defining their wants and making specific plans to fulfill them, clients previously feeling disengaged for the above reasons or for any other reason gain a sense of inner control. They begin to see their locus of control as internal rather than external. As Morales (1995) states, "When people see themselves as responsible for their actions . . . they stop paying attention to the casual opinions of others and evaluate what has been wrong (ineffective) about their own actions" (p. 6).

A major trend in the helping professions is the need for therapists to be culturally competent and to use evidence-based methods. In describing the interface of evidence-based methodologies and cultural competence, Whaley and Davis (2007) state, "Common elements of empirically supported treatment are the following: Treatment is short term; the emphasis is present focused and problem focused; skills training is stressed; the therapeutic relationship is considered to be important; and homework is assigned" (p. 572). Reality therapy includes the above elements and their adaptation to minorities and, in fact, to all clients.

Maya Angelou (2009) has said, "Human beings are more alike than we are unalike." Choice theory explains what makes us alike, and reality therapy, artfully applied, provides a bridge connecting therapists to individuals in their uniqueness and diversity.

INTERNATIONAL APPLICATIONS

The multicultural nature of reality therapy is evidenced by research, training programs, or reality therapy associations emerging from many countries such as Australia, Canada, Colombia, India, Iran, Israel, Japan, Kenya, Korea, Kuwait, Malaysia, New Zealand, Singapore, South Africa, and Taiwan and in seven European Union countries: Bosnia-Herzegovina, Croatia, Finland, Germany, Great Britain, Ireland, and Slovenia. Representatives from many countries come together at the international conference each year to exchange ideas, discuss current research projects, and learn cultural adaptations of choice theory and reality therapy.

The principles underlying choice theory as well as the theory itself are universal in that they explain human behavior and provide tools for enhancing mental health. Theoretical applications vary according to individual personalities, communication styles, and cultural characteristics. For instance, a Japanese person's application of the theory is often more indirect than that of an American. Asking a Japanese client, "What do you want?" can be perceived as intrusive. Consequently, this question is more appropriately formulated as, "What are you looking for" or "What are you seeking?" (Kakitani, 2009). Similarly, asking questions about the family's perception of an individual's situation carries more weight for a Singaporean therapist than for one whose culture is North American. Germans learning choice theory have expressed concern about the use of the words "control" and "power." Power is best described as strength (*starke*), potency or might (*macht*), or ability or mastery, as in being able (*konnen*) (Imhof, 2009). Some reality therapists are directive in their use of theory and practice; others more reflective and nonassertive. Some unwaveringly adhere to the language of internal control. Others use the language of clients and gradually lead them to incorporate internal control language. Wubbolding (2000a) states, "The delivery system, rooted in the bedrock of choice theory, lends itself to an unlimited number of personal enunciations" (p. 160).

RESEARCH EVIDENCE

Among the popular misconceptions about reality therapy is that it lacks research evidence supporting its validity. While more research is necessary, the effectiveness of reality therapy in many settings is well established. It has been studied in schools, in addictions programs, with prisoners, with juvenile delinquents, in relation to various mental health issues, and especially with multicultural groups on an international basis.

Criminal Justice

Lojk (1986) conducted follow-up studies of former prisoners over 12 years in Visnja Gora, Yugoslavia, when the country was still socialist. He found almost complete resocialization—that is, complete rehabilitation for 69%

of the former prisoners and partial success for 15%. The remaining 16% could not be contacted or were not rehabilitated. Lojk states:

> We felt these results were very promising. Unfortunately, some influential people didn't share our opinion. They were very skeptical about the sincerity of the social workers who gathered the data for the follow up study, and about our objectivity. The skeptics acknowledged that the released residents were no longer stealing; they had abandoned promiscuity; they were earning money for themselves and their children; they didn't change jobs more often than usual; they had no trouble with the police; and they didn't need any psychological or psychiatric help. However, the skeptics challenged the results and methodology of our study with the following arguments and questions: "The former residents seem O.K. but who knows?" "Are they internally happy?" "Could it mean that these methods of correction had broken their will for life?" Here you can see major misunderstandings about total behavior. (p. 30)

Angry Adolescents: Group Home

A not-so-congenial, challenging learning-centered modification of reality therapy used at the John Dewey Academy, a residential school for angry adolescents in Great Barrington, Massachusetts, has shown notable results. According to Collabolletta, Gordon, and Kaufman (2000), "Before admission 25% of the students had been hospitalized for at least two months, 75% had been treated by psychiatrists and 50% arrived addicted to potent psychotropic medication" (p. 42). Their diagnoses include attention deficit hyperactivity disorder, conduct disorder, oppositional defiance, substance abuse, and sociopathic disorders. Bratter, Collabolletta, Gordon, and Kaufman (1999) reported that of 313 students, 28% graduated and 75% of those who left received permission from their parents to return home. They state, "Two crucial statistics are: 100% of the graduates attend colleges of quality and 80% complete their higher education" (p. 11). Bratter (2008) states, "Since the first class graduated in 1987 all graduates have attended college . . . all but one of the class of 2006 made the Dean's List. The lowest average was 3.3" (p. 2). Of special interest and with some controversy, the

John Dewey Academy vigorously rejects the use of psychotropic medicine, asserting that

> personality and affective disorders rarely are cured by medicinal approaches. There is no pill that teaches self-respect and cures noxious narcissism, dishonesty and anti-social attitudes. Therefore, we eschew the use of psychotropic medications at JDA and view drug-free as a viable treatment goal. (Bratter, Esparat, Kaufman, & Sinsheimer, 2008, p. 22)

They cite as added success that members of the class of 2008 have been admitted to such universities as Brandeis, Oberlin, Sarah Lawrence, and the University of Chicago. They emphasize that this controversial system warrants further research and evaluation with various populations.

Group Homes: Quebec, Canada

Marcotte and Bilodeau (2007), working with Le Centre Jeunesse de Québec Scientific Research Team in conjunction with Laval University, reported on the effectiveness of reality therapy in four group homes for 5 years. As a result of intensive training, the youth workers were able to reduce the number of physical restraint incidents from 396 to 23 over that period. The researchers further observe that in their view "the mental and physical health of the teams (Youth Workers) is improving. Fewer sick days were taken with fewer workers suffering burnout. . . . Many admit to having more success and being happier at work" (p. 1).

Juvenile Delinquents

The effect of reality therapy with a juvenile delinquent population in Hong Kong showed a significant increase in self-esteem and a lessening of irresponsible behaviors. Using the Hudson inventory and relying on staff members' reports, participants showed definite improvements in punctuality, problem solving, and communication skills. Chung (1994) describes one especially memorable incident: Two boys from the treatment group refused to escape with 12 others from the same dormitory. Later they discussed how they chose to act appropriately after giving consideration to the escape plan. They stated that they decided to put into operation the principles they learned in the reality therapy group.

The participants' self-reports showed that among their changed behaviors were improvement in self-understanding, appreciation of their families, and gains in self-confidence and problem solving. Finally, an astonishing 65% wanted the group therapy sessions to increase from 12 to 20 weekly sessions.

Locus of Control

Finnerty (2007) investigated the effects of a 30-hour training program in choice theory on the locus of control and self-esteem of 30 adults ages 25 to 44 in a government-funded Community Employment Project in Dublin, Ireland. The focus of the agency is on helping jobless and socially excluded individuals gain work experience. Measurements contrasted internal locus of control with control by others and control by fate or chance. A pre- and post-training analysis of the data supported an increase in the internal locus of control and global self-worth scores at the significance level of $p < .0005$ level. Finnerty states, "The hypotheses that there would be a statistically significant increase in internal locus of control scores and global self-worth scores . . . were supported" (p. 34).

Korean Studies

The most extensive reality therapy research continues to emerge from Korea under the direction of Professor Rose-Inza Kim, dean (retired) at Sogang University in Seoul, Korea. She has facilitated 250 studies of reality therapy and choice theory between 1986 and 2006. Kim and Hwang (2006) conducted a meta-analysis of 43 studies addressing self-esteem and locus of control and found that, compared with the control group, 23% of the experimental group members increased their self-esteem and 28% scored higher on a measure of internal locus of control. The authors conclude that reality therapy and choice theory group programs "are effective for improving self-esteem and internal locus of control" (p. 29). They add, "This research could contribute to a baseline model to study and develop further group counseling programs using reality therapy and choice theory in Korea" (p. 29).

Mental Health Workers: Malaysia

In a study of the use of reality therapy among Malaysian mental health workers, Jazimin Jusoh, Mahmud, and Mohd Ishak (2008) found reality therapy applicable in the Malaysian context when consideration is given to various beliefs and backgrounds of clients: "The eastern culture which emphasizes close relationships, authoritative orientation, large family structure, dependency on each other, loyal, collaborative, harmonious, emotional control, and conservatism is different from the individualistic western culture" (p. 11). The main adjustment lies in the process of self-evaluation, which requires a balance between personal satisfaction and group harmony.

High School Classroom

Hinton and Warnke (2008) conducted a study (not yet finalized) in a suburban high school on the effect of choice theory and the WDEP system with students in the freshman class who had approximately the same grade point average. They divided the class into three teams with approximately the same number of students on each team. A comparison of the three teams revealed that the team whose teachers utilized choice theory and reality therapy in their classrooms had 29 referrals to the principal's office for disrespect, disruption, or vulgarity. Teachers from the other team referred students 95 times for similar offenses. Preliminary results from the remaining data point toward encouraging outcomes from the use of reality therapy in classroom management.

In-School Support Room

Passaro, Moon, Wiest, and Wong (2004) studied the effect of reality therapy used in an in-school support room (time-out room) for students in Grades 6 through 8. These students qualified as emotionally disturbed as described by the State of California Educational Code: "A condition exhibiting one or more characteristics, which exist over a long period of time and to a marked degree, which in turn adversely affects educational performance" (p. 505). All students met the criteria for attention-deficit/hyperactivity disorder (ADHD). Most students also qualified as having oppositional defiant disorder (ODD). The authors stated,

> Results were measured in three domains: changes in daily behavioral ratings over the school year; changes in the numbers of out of school suspensions compared to the previous academic year; and changes in the amount of time students participated in general education courses, within the current school year. (p. 508) Results showed that their daily behavioral rating improved by an average of 42%. Also, their combined participation in general education courses increased to over 62%. Furthermore, their out-of-school suspensions decreased by 12%. In summarizing the study, Passaro (personal communication, October 30, 2009) states, "Reality therapy is widely regarded by professionals working with oppositional and defiant youth as one of a few highly effective methodologies that can be successfully employed with this treatment resistant population."

Chronically Mentally Ill: Anecdote

While not qualifying as scientific research, the following anecdote illustrates the impact of reality therapy described by Witt (personal communication, September 30, 2008), who works for a mental health agency dealing with people the state or county considers "chronically and persistently mentally ill"—that is, people requiring care and treatment for their own welfare or for the welfare of others. Mental illness means a substantial disorder of thought, mood, perception, orientation, or memory that seriously impairs behavioral functioning and ability to cope with the ordinary demands of life. Many of Witt's clients have been in state mental hospitals for 15 or more years or are placed in her program as a last chance prior to institutionalization.

In her annual review Witt's supervisor said, "Although we aren't doing a controlled study the consumers that you are working with and using reality therapy with have shown sustained changes in their lives" (Witt, personal communication, September 30, 2008). Witt describes an individual considered to be a "lost cause" by the county who had been self-harming daily and hospitalized five times over a 6-month period and appeared to be headed for a state mental hospital within a month. As a result of her exposure to reality therapy, she has not been institutionalized and has reduced the number and severity of self-harming actions. She has improved her parenting skills and has not slapped her children in months while living in her own home with one night away for a respite.

Another client on Witt's case load was labeled a definite no-show. The therapist was told the client would never even come in for an interview. The client believed she was possessed and saw evil spirits while suffering from night paralysis. For many years she had been using drugs and alcohol and engaging in unsafe sexual practices as well as neglecting her children. From the time she began reality therapy approximately 12 months previously, she has been abstinent for 6 months and abstains from unsafe sexual practices. Though she occasionally talks about evil spirits, she evaluates her own behavior more effectively and has custody of her son 50% of the time. In the course of a year, she has missed only one appointment.

INNER MOTIVATION

The research studies and applications emphasized in this chapter focus on the efficacy and universal applicability of reality therapy. Additionally, other research studies corroborate the validity of principles underlying choice theory such as the inner motivation of human beings vs. the merit of external rewards. For example, Deci (1995) provided a research basis for internal motivation and, more specifically, the human need system. He states that his work "indicates that self-motivation, rather than external motivation, is at the heart of creativity, responsibility, healthy behavior and lasting change" (p. 9). For instance, his research shows that students doing specific tasks "just for the fun of it" were more likely to continue the work than students doing the tasks for pay. In describing *self-determination theory* (SDT), Ryan and Deci (2008) state that human beings "are understood to have basic psychological needs for autonomy, competence and relatedness, the satisfaction of which is essential for optimal development and mental health" (p. 190). This formulation of human motivation seems to be similar to the choice theory system of needs: freedom (autonomy), power (competence), and belonging (relatedness). They add, "The etiology of a wide number of psychological problems and psychotherapies lies in the dynamics of need depravation or thwarting during development" (p. 190).

TWO TYPES OF RESEARCH

None of the research studies cited in this chapter is perfectly designed. In the opinion of this author, "perfect design" is an oxymoron. Every research study is subject to limitations and criticism. Nevertheless, this small sample of studies conducted on the effectiveness of reality therapy serves as an illustration of its widespread use and applicability. Wubbolding (2000a) states:

> There are two kinds of research: cerebral research and fire in the belly research. The former consists of the many scientific studies on any topic or discipline on the premise that the proponents of any theory are accountable to the extent that they can demonstrate and validate their system empirically ... (however), the kind of research that will lead you the reader to embrace the principles and techniques of reality therapy is not scientific empiricism. The most persuasive documentation is the fire in the belly research. (p. 203)

When therapists personally witness a client sustaining even *one* dramatic change in behavior or leading a life characterized by healthy and effective choices, the result is a personal belief in the validity of the theory and the efficacy of the method used as well as self-confidence in using it. This "fire in the belly" or personal belief in reality therapy or in any other therapy does not create a valid system. Yet this personal experience can result in a desire to conduct empirical studies. Only the existence of scientific empirical studies elevates the theory and method and provides respectability in the professional community. The literature on reality therapy, illustrated in this sample of research studies, authenticates it as a credible system. Additionally, the endorsement by the European Association of Psychotherapy, the premier association of therapists throughout Europe, in 2008 has attested to reality therapy as a scientifically validated modality. The significance of this acknowledgement is explained in Chapter 6.

6

Future Developments

Reality therapy has long been associated with the name William Glasser. As founder and chief architect of reality therapy, he will be known in the history of our profession as the prime mover who has led his institute and inspired the work of practitioners and instructors. Believing that people choose their behavior and are driven by current motivations rather than external forces has required unceasing effort and unswerving commitment. At the same time, as with other theories of psychotherapy, reality therapy extends beyond one person's reach. Wubbolding and Brickell (2000) state,

> There is no doubt that to teach reality therapy is to teach the ideas of the founder. Still, reality therapy and The William Glasser Institute are not cults. Others have contributed to the expansion and application of reality therapy. Several significant events point toward the future status of reality therapy. The system is wider than even the charismatic personality of one man. (p. 65)

GLASSER SCHOLARS PROGRAM

To increase the research base and enhance the credibility of reality therapy, The William Glasser Institute adopted a proposal presented by Emerson Capps Dean at Midwestern University in Wichita Falls, Texas. Sixteen university professors were elected on a competitive basis to receive scholarships for the entire certification process, including tuition for training workshops as well as practica fees. Their participation in this process includes a commitment to conduct publishable research for the purpose of increasing the credibility of reality therapy. They represent a variety of professional disciplines—psychology, counseling, and social work—and are employed by universities in the United States and Australia.

EUROPEAN ASSOCIATION FOR PSYCHOTHERAPY (EAP): ENDORSEMENT

One of the most significant developments and advances in reality therapy is its recognition by the European Association for Psychotherapy (EAP). Founded in 1991, the EAP holds as one primary aim uniting psychotherapy organizations into a common association. For 8 years, the European Association for Reality Therapy (EART), under the skillful and determined leadership of Leon Lojk, psychologist in Slovenia, had prepared for this prestigious endorsement of reality therapy by the EAP. At its meeting in Tirana, Albania, the EAP recognized reality therapy as a scientifically validated psychotherapy. At this meeting the EART was recognized as a European Wide Organization (EWO). Prerequisites for this recognition are the scientific validation of the therapy and the existence of six national associations. The EART has organizations in Bosnia-Herzegovina, Croatia, Ireland, Finland, Great Britain, and Slovenia (Lojk, 2009; Wubbolding, 2009b).

The next and final level of recognition occurred in Brussels, Belgium, where the EAP officially accredited and endorsed the EART as a European Wide Awarding Organization (EWAO) within the EAP. At this meeting, the well-prepared ad hoc committee of EART, led by Leon Lojk and assisted by Boba Lojk, also of Slovenia, John Brickell of the United Kingdom, and Arthur Dunne and Jimmie Woods of Ireland, made their final presentation to the 30-member panel of the European Wide Organizations Committee (EWOC). After Lojk's presentation, the ad hoc committee was asked to leave the room while the EWOC committee members made their final decision. When the reality therapy ad hoc committee returned to the room they were greeted with enthusiastic applause signifying a vigorous endorsement.

This endorsement allows the EART to award the European Certificate in Psychotherapy (ECP) to those completing training in reality therapy beyond reality therapy certification. To achieve the ECP, a candidate must have a university degree (or equivalent) in the human or social sciences; achieve reality therapy certification; work with people who need psychotherapeutic interventions; and complete an additional 3-year training program in reality therapy, which includes 300 sessions of theory, 170 sessions of training in therapeutic skills, 1,150 hours work with clients, 200 hours of supervision, and 250 sessions of personal therapy and personal development experiences.

The importance of this event in the history of reality therapy cannot be overestimated. This major historic endorsement takes reality therapy to a higher level of prestige. The EAP represents 120,000 psychotherapists in 41 European countries, including 27 European Union countries. It has 28 national umbrella organizations and 18 European associations for psychotherapy and is a member of the World Council for Psychotherapy; it is also a non-governmental organization with consultative status with the Council of Europe. The endorsement of EART represents the culmination of many years of unfaltering commitment by Lojk, the ad hoc committee as well as many additional reality therapy associates.

LOYOLA MARYMOUNT UNIVERSITY

Two years of dialogue between Loyola Marymount University (LMU) in Los Angeles and The William Glasser Institute about preserving the work of Dr. Glasser and planning for the future of choice theory and reality therapy resulted in the formation of The William Glasser Institute for Research in Public Mental Health. The goal of the LMU Institute is to promote, study, and research the implications of mental health as a public issue. A major emphasis will center on research across 12 dimensions: counseling and therapy; relationships; quality schools; business and management; child advocacy; criminal justice and corrections; volunteerism and giving; addictions; violence, abuse, and trauma; health and wellness; ministry and faith traditions; and world peace and global relations.

Other initiatives include infusing choice theory and practice at the university, training faculty and staff, and establishing a professorship dedicated to research and public mental health. These challenging and futuristic goals are congruent with the university mission and spring from the mission of The William Glasser Institute. Leading this visionary program are Cheryl Grills, chair of the Department of Psychology, and Bradley Smith, Special Programs Coordinator.

INTERNATIONAL JOURNAL OF CHOICE THEORY AND REALITY THERAPY

In 1981 Larry Litwack founded and served as editor-in-chief of the *Journal of Reality Therapy* until 2010. In 1997 because of the growing number of international contributions, the editor added *International* to the title. The mission of the *International Journal of Reality Therapy* was "directed to the concepts of internal control psychology, with particular emphasis on research, theory, development or special descriptions of the successful application of internal control systems especially as exemplified by reality therapy and choice theory." Approximately 10% of articles focus on research, with others discussing applications, professional issues and skill development. In 2010 under the editorship of Thomas Parish, the journal has been renamed the *International Journal of Choice Theory and Reality Therapy* and is now published on-line.

EMPHASIS ON EMPIRICAL RESEARCH: RECOMMENDATIONS

Because reality therapy has appealed to practitioners more than to academics, empirical studies have been fewer in number than desired. Nevertheless, studies validating reality therapy are increasing in number, as indicated in Chapter 5. In summarizing six studies on reality therapy in schools, Murphy (1997) recommended the following:

- conducting more tightly controlled studies on reality therapy;
- gathering empirical evidence (in schools, measures should include grades, attendance, test scores and behavioral check lists);
- ensuring that "all persons who administer assessments or act as observers would be professionally trained and qualified for their specific tasks" (p. 19); and
- providing that "future research should be longitudinal lasting a full school year" (p. 19).

These recommendations aim at satisfying the ethical code for psychologists. According to Section 2.04 of the "Ethical Principles of Psychologists and Code of Conduct" (American Psychological Association, 2002), "Psychologists' work is based upon established scientific and professional knowledge of the discipline."

More specifically, this author urges researchers to consider the following recommendations for future research:

- In studying the effectiveness of reality therapy, genuine applications of the WDEP system should be emphasized. Spin-off systems or distorted forms of reality therapy do not qualify as genuine reality therapy.
- Part of research reports should include the amount of training provided for the persons using reality therapy. The William Glasser Institute sponsors an 18-month training and certification program in reality therapy. Some research studies have been conducted on programs led by individuals with considerably less training. This limitation in the research design should be clearly stated.
- Because many conflicts and disturbances require a protracted period for clients to alter their thinking and acting, a sufficient amount of time should be allotted for the research study to have credibility. Cognitive–behavioral therapists often state that 16 sessions are needed for significant results. While reality therapy is a stand-alone method, it is often placed in the cognitive school of therapy.

- Much reality therapy research has focused on the quality school philosophy and delivery system developed by Glasser (1990, 1993). Yet, as Wubbolding (2000a) states: "The training of the school staff has been sporadic, irregular, and inconsistent" (p. 233). The entire school staff should have at least some exposure to choice theory, the WDEP (wants, doing, self-evaluation, and planning) system of reality therapy, and "lead management" (i.e., reality therapy applied to school classrooms). A core group of faculty members should have achieved certification in reality therapy.
- As with research on many psychotherapy methods, more outcome research will enhance credibility. More studies should be conducted on behavioral incidents and academic achievement in school as well as recidivism in corrections, relapse in drug abuse, and mental disorders. The benchmark study conducted by Lojk (1986) on former prisoners could be replicated, as well as studies on juvenile delinquency (Chung, 1994), bullying (Kim, 2006), and drug addiction (Honeyman, 1990).

For enhanced credibility and continued improvement of school and agency programs using reality therapy, independent researchers should be involved. Independent evaluation precludes the criticism of self-studies that "the home team always wins"—that is, the results of self-studies are slanted toward a favorable outcome.

Looking to the future, Wubbolding delivered a major address at the 2009 international conference of The William Glasser Institute in Edinburgh, Scotland. He outlined reasons that reality therapy should be taught as a major system in psychology, counseling, social work, criminal justice, and other university programs. If reality therapy and perhaps any therapeutic theory is to flourish five conditions must be met:

1. A credible and comprehensive theory supporting a delivery system. Choice theory fulfills this condition. It is understandable, applicable to all areas of mental health, and multiculturally adaptable.
2. A delivery system that is usable and can be integrated into other systems. The WDEP system, with its emphasis on current wants and behaviors along with the major component of self-evaluation and

planning whereby clients conduct a searching self-assessment fol-lowed by specific plans, fulfills this condition. Reality therapy allows for placing emphasis on various components of human behavior: action, cognition, and feelings. Thus to some extent, it shares a com-mon border with person-centered therapy and cognitive therapy.

3. An organization of committed and dedicated individuals as well as regional and national associations. The William Glasser Institute, with its president, executive director, director of training, and board of advisors, has branches throughout the world on every continent except Antarctica. These branches are represented by delegates at the annual international convention. Individuals attend this convention from Africa, Asia, Australia, Europe, the Middle East, North America, and South America.

4. A clearly defined, respectable, and flexible training program con-ducted by qualified faculty. At the request of persons attending training programs, The William Glasser Institute developed a certification program in 1975. This program continues to evolve and gain prestige, as evidenced by the endorsement of the European Association for Psychotherapy, the Glasser Scholars Program, and the Loyola Marymount research center. Instructors with at least a master's degree who have completed a minimum of 2 years training beyond certification teach the training program.

5. Evidence of effectiveness. Even as more research is under way, reality therapy has been shown to be effective in a variety of settings. Some such studies are referenced in Chapter 5; others are described in the *International Journal of Reality Therapy* as well as in other sources (Wubbolding, 2000a).

Choice theory and reality therapy are best seen as open-ended sys-tems allowing for the incorporation of a variety of theoretical principles or practical techniques. Future developments will undoubtedly address the possible addition of a need for faith or spirituality as well as purpose and meaning. The incorporation of specific self-talk, both effective and ineffective, opens avenues for counseling beyond the exclusive discussion of actions (Wubbolding, 2000a). Adding perceived locus of control to the perceptual system builds on reality therapy as an internal control system (Mearns, 2008). Extending quality world wants by identifying their levels of intensity adds a concept to choice theory as a motivational system. Articulating specific forms of self-evaluation helps establish the centrality of the self-assessment process and affirms the theory as a freestanding system. The task of future researchers and practitioners will be to strike a balance between maintaining an open system while acknowledging the uniqueness of choice theory and reality therapy.

MENTAL HEALTH AS A PUBLIC HEALTH ISSUE

Even more basic are applications based on the therapists' and clients' perceptions of two general therapeutic pathways. In general, the therapy process can focus on remediation or on growth. Remediation implies focusing on problems by asking clients whether they want to abandon them and whether their ineffective behavior is helping or hurting in the pursuit of their goals. Growth-centered reality therapy focuses on existing strengths, including questions about positive qualities that can be increased and serve as a replacement for deficits. Questions focus on past or current successful choices with reflection on resulting positive feelings and need satisfaction. Because many presenting issues, even serious diagnosable conditions, are relationship-based, an effective pathway includes discussion of how to develop better interpersonal relationships with other significant people.

Building on reality therapy as a growth-centered system, Glasser has significantly extended the viewpoint that reality therapy is more than conventional psychotherapy. Though Glasser is widely known as the founder of reality therapy, his work has impacted not only the world of counseling and psychotherapy but also education, corrections, parenting, management, and supervision. He recently expressed the desire that his legacy include and even emphasize his impact on public health (Glasser, 2009). Just as clean water, the dangers of smoking, and many other topics are public health issues, Glasser views mental health as a public health issue. As is often the case, his viewpoints are controversial and arouse heated discussion. He emphasizes that physicians are not educators and the education of the public occupies *the* central place in bringing better mental health to the community. In rejecting the medical model of emphasizing mental disorders, Glasser states (2005a), "The cause of almost all public mental health problems is unhappiness . . . for example, almost half the people who get married divorce and we all are aware of many unhappily married people who never get a divorce" (pp. 15–16). He adds that unhappy relationships are the result of people unsuccessfully attempting to control others. Consequently, replacing the worldview based on external control with choice theory and the delivery system reality therapy is the highway to happiness and to reducing human conflict.

More specifically, focus groups studying choice theory as an educational process led by therapists or laypeople might serve as a way to prevent strife and increase happiness, especially in families. Glasser urges mental health associations, private counseling services, university health clinics and other agencies, and especially public schools to learn choice theory and how to implement it. He concludes that choice theory "is easy to teach, pleasant to learn and most people find it very useful" (2005a, p. 34).

With the desire that his major contribution rests with the concept "Public Mental Health," Glasser has expressed this hope for the future in his lectures and recent writing. Nevertheless, it is the belief of the author that his even greater contribution will be the founding and development of reality therapy that has always served as a mental health system more than a system used exclusively with mental disorders.

7

Summary

Reality therapy, formerly seen as the methodology of one man, founder William Glasser, is more appropriately described as a system or a school of thought. Glasser's monumental contribution serves as a foundation and an inspiration for professionals around the world who seek practical and proven skills for assisting clients. He continues to expand his original ideas and seeks to use reality therapy to strengthen human relationships, especially applied to the unique intimacy of marriage. If there could be one goal and one root cause of happiness, it would be better interpersonal relationships. Glasser and others have demonstrated a consistent effort to teach reality therapy as an antidote to poisonous societal influences undermining healthy relationships at work, at play, and in the home. His vision includes individuals adopting the principles of choice theory and reality therapy, thereby seeing their behavior as controlled from within. They are then willing to relinquish control of other people while extending a helping hand to them. The converse of this vision, attempting to control other people, is doomed to failure, creates unhappiness, and leads to ineffective and often harmful behaviors such as those described in the *Diagnostic and Statistical Manual*.

As an alternative to external control psychology, which is deplored by Glasser throughout his writings, internal control psychology, or choice theory, goes hand in hand with its delivery vehicle, the WDEP (wants, doing, self-evaluation, and planning) system of reality therapy. Clients influenced by societal values often ascribe responsibility for current behavior backward to childhood influences or trauma. Sometimes they project responsibility to their environment, especially to the coercive and external controlling behavior of other people. The reality therapist, while shunning blame and criticism, helps clients focus on their current wants, behavior, and plans. Throughout the therapeutic process clients conduct a serious and often courageous self-evaluation directed toward the attainability of their wants and the effectiveness and reasonableness of their actions. This ongoing assessment, a *sine qua non*, of the efficacious use of reality therapy has many manifestations such as: "Is what you're doing helping you?" "Is what you are doing helping or hurting others?" "Will your current actions get you what you want?" "Are your wants realistically attainable?" "If they're fulfilled, will they contribute to or diminish your need fulfillment or that of others?" "How does it help you to tell yourself that you are powerless?" "What effect would the opposite self-talk have on your life direction?" "Are your plans realistically doable and how much are you committed to following through?"

As a system, reality therapy is now supported by research studies as well as by the witness of therapists from virtually every continent. Ongoing expanded research will continue to enhance and develop reality therapy as well as encourage new followers and practitioners. Specific suggestions for further studies are discussed in Chapter 5.

Finally, after completing this book, I suggest you return to Chapter 3 and review your interpretation of the behavior of Noel, the college student. Has your explanation changed? Are you able to use the language of internal control psychology? Are you able to use the language of choice theory and reality therapy in explaining the events? And most importantly, how would you use the WDEP system with Noel?

Appendix: Exploring Wants

CATEGORIES OF WANTS	QUESTIONS FOR EACH CATEGORY
A. Family	What do I want that I am getting?
B. Spouse	What do I want that I'm NOT getting?
C. Children	How much do I want it?
D. Friends	How much effort or energy am I
E. Job	willing to exert to get what I want?
F. Manager	What will I settle for?
G. Subordinates	What am I getting that I *don't* want?
H. The Organization	What are the priorities in what I want?
(religious, civic, etc.)	What is my level of commitment?
I. Coworkers	How do I perceive the categories listed?
J. Recreational activities	What needs to be done, regardless of
K. Myself	whether I want to do it?
L. Therapist	

Glossary of Key Terms

CHOICE THEORY   The underlying justification for reality therapy, an internal control psychology stating that human behavior originates from within the person and is not the result of external stimuli, environment, or personal past experiences. Human behavior springs from five genetic needs: survival or self-preservation, love or belonging, power or inner control, freedom or independence, and fun or enjoyment.

PERCEIVED WORLD   The collection of images, which may include desirable, undesirable, and neutral images.

PERCEPTION   The input received from the external world, resulting from behavioral choices and made up of the perceived world and perceptual filters.

PERCEPTUAL FILTERS   Lenses through which human beings see the world and place values on input or information received from it.

QUALITY WORLD   The collection of specific wants and desires as well as mental pictures of everything and everyone having high value—that is, satisfying the five genetic needs of choice theory. The quality world constitutes the proximate source of motivation.

REALITY THERAPY   Founded by William Glasser, MD, in the 1960s in a mental hospital and a correctional institution, constituting a therapeutic system in which clients are asked to discuss their current behaviors with the goal of formulating more need satisfying choices. These choices aim at satisfying the five needs described in choice theory as well as the reasonable expectations of society.

TONIC BEHAVIORS   Relationship behaviors that bring people closer together. Used in therapy, they facilitate the therapeutic alliance.

TOTAL BEHAVIOR   The collection of actions, cognition, emotions, and physiology generated by specific unfulfilled wants, with the most direct control of actions and cognition. All behaviors contain all four components.

TOXIC BEHAVIOR   Behaviors that create a poisonous atmosphere in human relationships. If used in therapy, they damage the relationship and impede therapeutic progress.

WDEP   The formulation of reality therapy with each letter representing a cluster of ideas and concepts as well as relevant questions designed to help therapists establish the therapeutic alliance with clients and connect with their internal motivation: W—wants, perceptions; D—doing (total behavior); E—self-evaluation; and P—plan of action.

Suggested Readings

Glasser, W. (1998). *Choice theory*. New York, NY: Harper Collins.

This detailed exposition of choice theory as the basis of reality therapy marks the change in the name of the theory from control theory to choice theory. It is a foundational book for students of reality therapy who desire an extended treatment of choice theory.

Glasser, W. (2005). *Defining mental health as a public health problem*. Los Angeles, CA: The William Glasser Institute.

This brief discussion lays out Glasser's attempt to redefine mental health as a public issue and to challenge the widespread use of psychiatric drugs. Glasser describes the implementation of choice theory as a pathway to better mental health.

Wubbolding, R. (2000). *Reality therapy for the 21st century*. Philadelphia, PA: Brunner Routledge.

This comprehensive and detailed treatment of reality therapy contains an overview of choice theory and several extensions of the theory. A major contribution of this book is the application to cross-cultural counseling: Japanese, Koreans, African Americans, Hispanics, Chinese, and others. The WDEP system empowers clients and provides an alternative to the victimization felt by many clients. This book is a basic source used in training programs as diverse as those in Korea, the United Kingdom, Kuwait, Singapore, and South Africa.

Wubbolding, R., & Brickell, J. (2001). *Counselling with reality therapy*. Bicester, Oxon, UK: Speechmark Publishing.

This book extends reality therapy to relationship counseling, stages of group counseling, and addictions counseling. Along with paradoxical techniques applied to resistance, additional topics are explained, such as using metaphors, listening for themes, and creating client anticipation.

Wubbolding, R., & Brickell J. (2001). *A set of directions for putting and keeping yourself together*. Minneapolis, MN: Educational Media.

This practical, hands-on source for self-help can be used with individual clients, students, and groups. Specific planning activities designed for each human need.

Ways to combat negative actions, thoughts, and feelings provide the reader with tools for self-help and for use with families. This book can be used in conjunction with an online program available through The William Glasser Institute.

FURTHER RESOURCES

Wubbolding, R. (2007). *Reality therapy* [DVD]. Washington, DC: American Psychological Association.

Robert Wubbolding counsels a client, applying the WDEP system to a 40-year-old man who gradually becomes aware of the impact of his harsh communication patterns with his girlfriend. The therapist helps him define and clarify his wants, evaluate his current interactions with her, and formulate specific plans for improving his communication to enhance their relationship. The therapist also illustrates how a paradoxical intervention, the double bind, is incorporated into reality therapy.

Wubbolding, R. (2008). *Reality therapy for addictions* [DVD]. Available from http://www.psychotherapy.net.

Robert Wubbolding counsels a client struggling with addiction. Complicated by depression, the client's recovery from cocaine addiction is laborious and challenging. The client is both cooperative and passively resistant. Jon Carlson and Judy Lewis conduct a detailed discussion with Dr. Wubbolding on choice theory and reality therapy.

The William Glasser Institute

To facilitate the lasting influence of reality therapy and to ensure that the essential principles endure in decades to come, Glasser founded this institute, originally known as the Institute for Reality Therapy. This organization sanctions an 18-month training program leading to certification, RTC (Reality Therapy Certified). Further training leads to status as a faculty member of The William Glasser Institute. For more information, contact:

The William Glasser Institute
22024 Lassen Street, Suite 118
Chatsworth, CA 91311
Tel: 1-800-899-0688
Fax: 1-818-700-0555
E-Mail: wginst@wglasser.com
Website: www.wglasser.com

Center for Reality Therapy

The Center for Reality Therapy under the direction of Robert E. Wubbolding, who is also the director of training for The William Glasser Institute, sponsors 1-day, 2-day, and 3-day workshops, the latter of which is applicable for certification through The William Glasser Institute. The mission of the Center is to teach reality therapy to an increasing number of persons who wish to make professional or personal applications.

Center for Reality Therapy

Robert E. Wubbolding, EdD, Director

7672 Montgomery Road #383

Cincinnati, OH 45236

Tel: 1-513-561-1911

Fax: 1-513-561-3568

E-Mail: wubsrt@fuse.net

Website: www.realitytherapywub.com

References

American Psychiatric Association. (2000). *Diagnostic and statistical manual of mental disorders (IV-TR)*. Washington, DC: Author.

American Psychological Association. (2002a). *Ethical principles of psychologists and code of conduct*. Washington, DC: Author.

American Psychological Association. (2002b). Guidelines on multicultural education, training, research, practice, and organizational change for psychologists. Retrieved from http://www.apa.org/practice/guidelines/multicultural.pdf

Angelou, M. (2009). Angelou never gave up hope [YouTube interview]. Retrieved from http://www.youtube.com/watch?v=lTCcOLWr7-s&feature=channel

Arbona, C., & Virella, B. (2008). Psychological issues with Puerto Ricans: A review of research findings. In C. Negy (Ed.), *Cross-cultural psychotherapy* (pp. 103–132). Reno, NV: Bent Tree Press.

Aurelius, M. (1944). *The meditations of Marcus Aurelius*. (A. Farquharson, Ed.). London, England: Oxford University Press.

Beck, A., & Weishaar, M. (2008). Cognitive therapy. In R. Corsini (Ed.), *Current psychotherapies* (8th ed., pp. 263–294). Belmont, CA: Thomson Brooks/Cole.

Bratter, T. (2008). *The John Dewey Academy flourishes*. Retrieved from http://www.strugglingteens.com/artman/publish/JohnDeweyAcademyBN_081118.shtml

Bratter, T., Collabolletta, E., Gordon, D., & Kaufman, S. (1999). *The John Dewey Academy: Motivating unconvinced, gifted, self-destructive adolescents to use their superior assets*. Unpublished manuscript.

Bratter, T., Esparat, D., Kaufman, A., & Sinsheimer, L. (2008). Confrontational psychotherapy: A compassionate and potent psychotherapeutic orientation for gifted adolescents who are self-destructive and engage in dangerous behavior. *International Journal of Reality Therapy, 27*(2), 13–25.

Britzman, M. J. (2009). *Pursuing the good life*. Bloomington, IN: Unlimited Publishing.

Buck, N. (2000). *Peaceful parenting*. San Diego, CA: Black Forest Press.

Burnett, D. (1995). *Raising responsible kids*. Laguna Nigel, CA: Funagain Press.

Carleton, R. (1994). Reality therapy in the Christian context [Audio cassette]. Montgomery, AL: Private Publication.

Carlson, J., & Englar-Carlson, M. (2008). Adlerian therapy. In J. Frew & M. Spiegler (Eds.), *Contemporary psychotherapies for a diverse world* (pp. 93–140). Boston, MA: Houghton Mifflin.

Cavanagh, J., & McGoldrick, J. (1953). *Fundamental psychiatry.* Milwaukee, WI: Bruce.

Cheng, N. (1986). *Life and death in Shanghai.* New York, NY: Grafton Books.

Chung, M. (1994). Can reality therapy help juvenile delinquents in Hong Kong? *Journal of Reality Therapy, 14*(1), 68–80.

Collabolletta, E., Gordon, D., & Kaufman, S. (2000). The John Dewey Academy: Motivating students to use, rather than abuse, their superior assets. *International Journal of Reality Therapy, 19*(2), 38–45.

Corey, G. (2009). *Theory and practice of counseling and psychotherapy* (8th ed.). Belmont, CA: Thomson Brooks/Cole.

Deci, E. (1995). *Why we do what we do.* New York, NY: Penguin Books.

Ellis, A. (2008). Rational emotive behavior therapy. In R. Corsini (Ed.), *Current psychotherapies* (8th ed., pp. 187–222). Belmont, CA: Thomson Brooks/Cole.

Ellis, A., & Harper, R. (1997). *A guide to rational living* (3rd ed.). North Hollywood, CA: Wilshire Books.

Ellsworth, L. (2007). *Choosing to heal.* New York, NY: Routledge.

Fajors, N., & Negy, C. (2008). African American clients: History and therapy considerations. In C. Negy (Ed.), *Cross-cultural psychotherapy* (pp. 161–185). Reno, NV: Bent Tree Press.

Feinauer, L., Mitchell, J., Harper, J., & Dane, S. (1998). The impact of hardiness and severity of childhood sexual abuse on adult adjustment. *The American Journal of Family Therapy, 24*(3), 206–214.

Finnerty, M. (2007). Choice theory training: Effects on locus of control and self-esteem in adult community employment workers. *International Journal of Choice Theory, 2*(1), 30–34.

Ford, E. (1979). *Permanent love.* Minneapolis, MN: Winston.

Frankl, V. (1984). *Man's search for meaning.* New York, NY: Washington Square Press.

Frew, J. (2008). Gestalt therapy. In J. Frew & M. Spiegler (Eds.), *Contemporary psychotherapies for a diverse world* (pp. 228–274). Boston, MA: Houghton Mifflin.

Frew, J., & Spiegler, M. (2008). Introduction to contemporary psychotherapies for a diverse world. In J. Frew & M. Spiegler (Eds.), *Contemporary psychotherapies for a diverse world* (pp. 1–19). Boston, MA: Houghton Mifflin.

Genetic Science Learning Center, University of Utah. (2008). *The new science of addiction: Genetics and the brain.* Retrieved from http://learn.genetics.utah.edu/units/addiction/

Gilchrist Banks, S. (2009). *Using choice theory and reality therapy to enhance student achievement and responsibility.* Alexandria, VA: American School Counselor Association.

Glasser, N. (Ed.). (1980). *What are you doing?* New York, NY: Harper & Row.

Glasser, N. (Ed.). (1989). *Control theory in the practice of reality therapy.* New York, NY: Harper & Row.

Glasser, W. (1960). *Mental health or mental illness?* New York, NY: Harper & Row.

Glasser, W. (1965). *Reality therapy.* New York, NY: Harper & Row.

Glasser, W. (1968). *Schools without failure.* New York, NY: Harper & Row.

Glasser, W. (1972). *The identity society.* New York, NY: Harper & Row.

Glasser, W. (1976). *Positive addiction.* New York, NY: Harper & Row.

Glasser, W. (1980). *Stations of the mind.* New York, NY: Harper & Row.

Glasser, W. (1984). *Control theory.* New York, NY: HarperCollins.

Glasser, W. (1990). *The quality school.* New York, NY: HarperCollins.

Glasser, W. (1993). *The quality school teacher.* New York, NY: HarperCollins.

Glasser, W. (1996, Summer). Dr. Glasser's Corner. *The William Glasser Institute Newsletter,* 3–4.

Glasser, W. (1998). *Choice theory.* New York, NY: HarperCollins.

Glasser, W. (2000a). *Reality therapy in action.* New York, NY: HarperCollins.

Glasser, W. (2000b). *Every student can succeed.* Chula Vista, CA: Black Forest Press.

Glasser, W. (2003). *Warning: Psychiatry can be hazardous to your mental health.* New York, NY: HarperCollins.

Glasser, W. (2005a). *Defining mental health as a public health issue.* Chatsworth, CA: The William Glasser Institute.

Glasser, W. (2005b). *How the brain works chart.* Chatsworth, CA: The William Glasser Institute.

Glasser, W. (2007). *Eight lessons for a happier marriage.* New York, NY: HarperCollins.

Glasser, W. (2008, July 16). *Back to the basics.* Keynote address to annual international conference of The William Glasser Institute, Colorado Springs, CO.

Glasser, W., & Glasser, C. (1999). *The language of choice theory.* New York, NY: HarperCollins.

Glasser, W., & Glasser, C. (2008, Summer). Procedures: The cornerstone of institute training. *The William Glasser Institute Newsletter,* 1.

Glasser, W., & Wubbolding, R. (1995). Reality therapy. In R. Corsini (Ed.), *Current psychotherapies* (5th ed., pp. 293–321). Itasca, IL: Peacock.

Glasser, W., & Zunin, L. (1973). Reality therapy. In R. Corsini (Ed.), *Current psychotherapies* (2nd ed., pp. 283–297). Itasca, IL: Peacock.

Greene, B. (1994). *New paradigms for creating quality schools.* Chapel Hill, NC: New View Publications.

Hawthorn, T. (2008, August 18). A golden day for a village that reached out to a family. *Globe and Mail,* pp. 1, 7.

Hirsch, J. (2004). *Two souls indivisible.* New York, NY: Houghton Mifflin.

Hoglund, R. (2007). *Intervention strategies: Educating for responsibility and quality.* Tempe, AZ: Hoglund.

Honeyman, A. (1990). Perceptual changes in addicts as a consequence of reality therapy based on group treatment. *Journal of Reality Therapy, 9*(2), 53–59.

Ivey, A. E., D'Andrea, M., Ivey, M. B., & Simek-Morgan, L. (2007). *Theories of counseling and psychotherapy: A multicultural perspective* (6th ed.). Boston, MA: Allyn & Bacon.

Jazimin Jusoh, A., Mahmud, Z., & Mohd Ishak, N. (2008). The patterns of reality therapy usage among Malaysian counselors. *International Journal of Reality Therapy, 28*(1), 5–14.

Kaiser, H. (1965). The problems of responsibility in psychotherapy. In B. Fierman (Ed.), *Effective psychotherapy* (pp. 1–13). New York, NY: Free Press.

Kim, J- U. (2006). The effect of a bullying prevention program on responsibility and victimization of bullied children in Korea. *Journal of Reality Therapy, 26*(1), 4–8.

Kim, R- I., & Hwang, M. (2006). A meta-analysis of reality therapy and choice theory group programs for self-esteem and locus of control in Korea. *International Journal of Choice Theory, 1*(1), 25–30.

Kratochwill, T., & Morris, R. (1993). *Handbook of psychotherapy with children and adolescents.* Boston, MA: Allyn & Bacon.

Lazarus, A. (2008). Multimodal therapy. In R. Corsini (Ed.), *Current psychotherapies* (8th ed., pp. 368–401). Belmont, CA: Thomson Brooks/Cole.

Linnenberg, D. (1997). Religion, spirituality in the counseling process. *International Journal of Reality Therapy, 17*(1), 55–59.

Litwack, L. (2005). Editor's comments. *International Journal of Reality Therapy, 24(2),* 3–4.

Litwack, L. (2007). Basic needs—a retrospective. *International Journal of Reality Therapy, 16*(2), 28–30.

Lojk, L. (1986). My experiences using reality therapy. *Journal of Reality Therapy, 5*(2), 28–35.

Lojk, L. (2009). 4th European international conference in Edinburgh. *International Journal of Reality Therapy, 29*(1), 30–33.

Luborsky, E., O'Reilly-Landry, M., & Arlow, J. (2008). Psychoanalysis. In R. Corsini (Ed.), *Current psychotherapies* (8th ed., pp. 15–62). Belmont, CA: Thomson Brooks/Cole.

MacColl, L. A. (1946). *Fundamental theory of servo-mechanism.* New York, NY: Van Nostrand.

Marcotte, C., & Bilodeau, S. (2007). Reality therapy and research in group homes project. Montreal, Quebec. Retrieved from http://www.centrejeunessedequebec .qc.ca/

Mearns, J. (2008). *The social learning theory of Julian B. Rotter.* Retrieved from http:// psych.fullerton.edu/jmearns/rotter.htm

Mendelowitz, E., & Schneider, K. (2008). Existential psychotherapy. In R. Corsini (Ed.), *Current psychotherapies* (8th ed., pp. 295–327). Belmont, CA: Thomson Brooks/Cole.

Theory. (n.d.). *Merriam-Webster online dictionary.* Retrieved from http://www .merriam-webster.com/dictionary/theory

Mickel, E. (2005). *Africa centered reality therapy and choice theory.* Trenton, NJ: Africa World Press.

Mickel, E., & Hall, C. (2006). Family therapy in transition: Love is a healing behavior. *International Journal of Reality Therapy, 15*(2), 32–35.

Mickel, L., & Liddie-Hamilton, B. (1996). Family therapy in transition: Social constructivism and control theory. *Journal of Reality Therapy, 16*(1), 95–100.

Moore, T. (1944). *Personal mental hygiene.* New York, NY: Grune & Stratton.

Morales, M. A. A. (1995). *Why reality therapy works for Puerto Ricans.* Unpublished manuscript; available from Box 4929, Hato Rey, Puerto Rico 00919.

Mosak, H., & Maniacci, M. (2008). Adlerian psychotherapy. In R. Corsini (Ed.), *Current psychotherapies* (8th ed., pp. 63–106). Belmont, CA: Thomson Brooks/Cole.

Murdock, N. (2004). *Theories of counseling and psychotherapy: A case approach.* Upper Saddle River, NJ: Merrill/Prentice Hall.

Murphy, L. (1997). Efficacy of reality therapy in the schools: A review of the research from 1980–1995. *Journal of Reality Therapy, 16*(2), 12–20.

Myers, L., & Jackson, D. (2002). *Realty therapy and choice theory.* Lanham, MD: American Correctional Association.

Negy, C. (2008). Treating dissimilar clients: No longer the road less traveled. In C. Negy (Ed.), *Cross-cultural psychotherapy* (pp. 3–22). Reno, NV: Bent Tree Press.

Okonji, J. (1995). Counseling style preference and perception of counselors by African American male students. *Dissertation Abstracts* B 55/09, 3811.

Okonji, J., Ososkie, J., & Pullos, S. (1996). Preferred style and ethnicity of counselors by African American males. *Journal of Black Psychology, 22*(3), 329–339.

Parish, J., & Parish, T. (1999). An examination of teacher caring, underachievement, and at-risk behaviors. *International Journal of Reality Therapy, 19*(1), 27–31.

Pask, G. (1976). *The cybernetics of learning and performance.* London, England: Hutchinson.

Passaro, P., Moon, M., Wiest, D., & Wong, E. (2004). A model for school psychology practice: Addressing the needs of students with emotional and behavioral challenges through the use of an in-school support room and reality therapy. *Adolescence, 39*(155), 503–517.

Patterson, C. H. (1974). *Relationship counseling.* New York, NY: HarperCollins.

Pierce, K. (2007). *Using lead management on purpose.* Lincoln, NE: iUniverse.

Pierce, K., & Taylor, A. (2008). *The dance of bullying.* Lincoln, NE: iUniverse.

Powers, W. (1973). *Behavior: The control of perception.* New York, NY: Aldine.

Primason, R. (2004). *Choice parenting.* Lincoln, NE: iUniverse.

Richardson, B. (2001). *Working with challenging youth.* Philadelphia, PA: Brunner-Routledge.

Roth, B., & Goldring, C. (2008). *Relationship counseling with choice theory strategies.* Beverly Hills, CA: Association of Ideas Publishing.

Rotter, J. B. (1954). *Social learning and clinical psychology.* New York, NY: Prentice Hall.

Roy, J. (2005). *Soul shapers.* Hagerstown, MD: Review and Herald.

Roy, J. (2006). *The development of the ideas of William Glasser: A biographical study.* Unpublished doctoral dissertation. La Sierra University, Riverside, CA.

Ryan, R., & Deci, E. (2008). A self-determination theory approach to psychotherapy: The motivational basis for effective change. *Canadian Psychology, 49*(3), 186–193.

Salzman, M. (2003). *True noteboooks.* New York, NY: Vintage Books.

Sharf, R. (2008). *Theories of psychotherapy and counseling: concepts and cases.* Belmont, CA: Thomson Brooks/Cole.

Sickles, W. (1976). *Psychology: A matter of mind.* Dubuque, IA: Kendall/Hunt.

Slavik, S., Sperry, L., & Carlson, J. (2000). Efficient Adlerian therapy with individuals and couples. In J. Carlson and L. Sperry (Ed.), *Brief therapy with individuals & couples* (pp. 248–263). Phoenix, AZ: Zeig, Tucker & Theisen.

Spiegler, M. (2008). Behavior therapy II: Cognitive-behavioral therapy. In J. Frew & M. Spiegler (Eds.), *Contemporary psychotherapies for a diverse world* (pp. 320–359). Boston, MA: Lahaska Press.

Staub, E., & Pearlman, L. (2002). Understanding basic psychological needs. Retrieved from http://www.heal-reconcile-rwanda.org/lec_needs.htm

Sue, D. W., & Sue, D. (1999). *Counseling the culturally different: Theory and practice* (3rd ed.). New York, NY: Wiley.

Sue, D. W., & Sue, D. (2003). *Counseling the culturally diverse: Theory and practice* (4th ed.). New York, NY: Wiley.

Sullo, R. (2007). *Activating the desire to learn.* Alexandria, VA: Association for Supervision and Curriculum.

Tabata, M. (1999). The usefulness of reality therapy for biblical counseling. *Japanese Journal of Reality Therapy, 5*(1), 30–34.

Talmon, M. (1990). *Single-session therapy.* San Francisco, CA: Jossey-Bass.

Webster's concise desk encyclopedia. (1995). New York, NY: Barnes & Noble Books.

Webster's New World College Dictionary (4th ed.). (1999). New York, NY: MacMillan.

Weinberg, G. (1985). *Secrets of consulting.* New York, NY: Dorset House.

Whaley, A., & Davis, K. (2007). Cultural competence and evidence-based practice in mental health services. *American Psychologist, 62*(6), 563–574.

Wiener, N. (1948). *Cybernetics.* New York, NY: Wiley.

Wiener, N. (1952). *Nonlinear problems in random theory.* New York, NY: Technology Press of MIT and Wiley.

The William Glasser Institute. (2005). *Programs, policies and procedures of the William Glasser Institute.* (2005). Chatsworth, CA: Author.

Wilson, L., & Stith, S. (1991). Culturally sensitive therapy with black clients. *Journal of Multicultural Counseling and Development, 19*(1), 32–43.

Wubbolding, R. (1988). *Using reality therapy.* New York, NY: Harper & Row.

Wubbolding, R. (1989). Radio station WDEP and other metaphors used in teaching reality therapy. *Journal of Reality Therapy, 8*(2), 74–79.

Wubbolding, R. (1990). Evaluation: The cornerstone in the practice of reality therapy. *Omar Psychological Series, 1*(2), 6–27.

Wubbolding, R. (1991). *Understanding reality therapy.* New York, NY: HarperCollins.

Wubbolding, R. (1992). *You steer* [CD]. Cincinnati, OH: Center for Reality Therapy.

Wubbolding, R. (1998). Client inner self-evaluation: A necessary prelude to change. In H. Rosenthal (Ed.), *Favorite counseling and therapy techniques* (pp. 196–197). Washington, DC: Taylor & Francis.

Wubbolding, R. (2000a). *Reality therapy for the 21st century*. Philadelphia, PA: Brunner Routledge.

Wubbolding, R. (2000b). Reality therapy. In A. Horne (Ed.), *Family counseling and therapy* (3rd ed., pp. 420–453). Itasca, IL: Peacock.

Wubbolding, R. (2003). Reality therapy theory. In D. Capuzzi (Ed.), *Counseling and psychotherapy* (3rd ed., pp. 255–282). Upper Saddle River, NJ: Merrill Prentice Hall.

Wubbolding, R. (2004). *You steer* [CD]. Cincinnati, OH: Center for Reality Therapy.

Wubbolding, R. (2005). The power of belonging. *International Journal of Reality Therapy, 24*(2), 43–44.

Wubbolding, R. (2006). Searching for mental health. *International Journal of Choice Theory, 1*(1), 5–6.

Wubbolding, R. (2007). Glasser quality school. *Group Dynamics: Theory, Research, and Practice, 11*(4), 253–261.

Wubbolding, R. (2008a). *Cycle of managing, supervising, counseling and coaching* (Chart, 16th revision). Cincinnati, OH: Center for Reality Therapy.

Wubbolding, R. (2008b). More searching for mental health. *International Journal of Choice Theory, 2*(1), 6–9.

Wubbolding, R. (2008c). Reality therapy. In J. Frew & M. Spiegler (Eds.), *Contemporary psychotherapies for a diverse world* (pp. 360–396). Boston, MA: Houghton Mifflin.

Wubbolding, R. (2009a). *Reality therapy training manual* (15th revision). Cincinnati, OH: Center for Reality Therapy.

Wubbolding, R. (2009b). 2029: Headline of footnote? Mainstream or backwater? Cutting edge or trailing edge? Included or excluded from the professional world? *International Journal of Reality Therapy, 29*(1), 26–29.

Wubbolding, R., & Brickell, J. (2000). Misconceptions about reality therapy. *International Journal of Reality Therapy, 19*(2), 64–65.

Wubbolding, R., & Brickell, J. (2001). *A set of directions for putting and keeping yourself together*. Minneapolis, MN: Educational Media.

Wubbolding, R., & Brickell, J. (2005). Purpose of behavior: Language and levels of commitment. *International Journal of Reality Therapy, 25*(1), 39–41.

Wubbolding, R., & Brickell, J. (2007). Frequently asked questions and brief answers: Part I. *International Journal of Reality Therapy, 27*(1), 29–30.

Wubbolding, R., Brickell, J., Imhof, L., Kim, R., Lojk, L., & Al-Rashidi, B. (2004). Reality therapy: A global perspective. *International Journal for the Advancement of Counselling, 26*(3), 219–228.

Wubbolding, R., Brickell, J., Loi, I., & Al-Rashidi, B. (2001). The why and how of self-evaluation. *International Journal of Reality Therapy, 21*(1), 36–37.

Yontef, G., & Jacobs. L. (2008). Gestalt therapy. In R. Corsini (Ed.), *Current psychotherapies* (8th ed., pp. 328–367). Belmont, CA: Thomson Brooks/Cole.

Index

About the Author

Robert E. Wubbolding, EdD, an internationally known teacher, author, and practitioner of reality therapy, teaches choice theory and reality therapy in the United States, Europe, Asia, and the Middle East. His contributions to theory and practice include the ideas of *positive symptoms, the cycle of counseling, five levels of commitment,* and others; he has also significantly expanded the procedure of *evaluation.* Dr. Wubbolding has written over 130 articles, essays, and chapters in textbooks, and completed 10 books and nine videos on reality therapy, including the widely acclaimed books *Reality Therapy for the 21st Century* and *A Set of Directions for Putting and Keeping Yourself Together.*

His busy professional life includes positions as director of the Center for Reality Therapy; Professor Emeritus at Xavier University in Cincinnati, Ohio; and senior faculty for The William Glasser Institute in Los Angeles, California. In 1987 he was personally appointed by Dr. Glasser to be the first director of training for the Institute. In this position he coordinates and monitors the certification, supervisor, and instructor training programs.

Dr. Wubbolding formerly consulted with the drug and alcohol abuse programs of the U.S. Army and Air Force. He has been a group counselor at a halfway house for women, an elementary and secondary school counselor, a high school teacher, and a teacher of adult basic education. For 2 years he taught for the University of Southern California in their overseas programs in Japan, Korea, and Germany.

His professional memberships include the American Counseling Association, the American Psychological Association, the American Mental Health Counseling Association, and many other national and state psychological and counseling associations. Dr. Wubbolding has received the following awards: the Marvin Rammelsberg Award, presented to a person in a helping profession best exemplifying qualities of friendship, brotherhood, and humanitarianism while displaying exemplary leadership qualities and making outstanding contributions to professional organizations; the Herman J. Peters Award, for exemplary leadership to promote the profession of counseling; the Greater Cincinnati Counseling Association Recognition of Merit Award; the Mary Corre Foster Award, for exemplifying qualities of leadership within the counseling profession and promoting the standards of excellence within the profession; Distinguished Alumnus Award, College of Education, University of Cincinnati, Ohio (2002); Distinguished Counseling Graduate of the 1970s, College of Education, University of Cincinnati, Ohio (2005); and the Gratitude Award for initiating reality therapy in the United Kingdom from the Institute for Reality Therapy, United Kingdom (2009).

> He is one of my closest and most trusted associates.
> I couldn't recommend anyone more highly.
> —William Glasser, MD, founder of reality therapy

About the Series Editors

Jon Carlson, PsyD, EdD, ABPP, is distinguished professor of psychology and counseling at Governors State University in University Park, Illinois, and a psychologist at the Wellness Clinic in Lake Geneva, Wisconsin. Dr. Carlson has served as the editor of several periodicals, including the *Journal of Individual Psychology* and *The Family Journal*. He holds diplomas in both family psychology and Adlerian psychology. He has authored 150 journal articles and 40 books, including *Time for a Better Marriage, Adlerian Therapy, The Mummy at the Dining Room Table, Bad Therapy, The Client Who Changed Me,* and *Moved by the Spirit*. He has created more than 200 professional trade videos and DVDs with leading professional therapists and educators. In 2004 the American Counseling Association named him a "Living Legend." Recently he syndicated the advice cartoon *On The Edge* with cartoonist Joe Martin.

Matt Englar-Carlson, PhD, is an associate professor of counseling at California State University, Fullerton, and an adjunct senior lecturer in the School of Health at the University of New England in Armidale, Australia. He is a fellow of Division 51 of the American Psychological Association (APA). As a scholar, teacher, and clinician, Dr. Englar-Carlson has been an innovator and is professionally passionate about training and teaching clinicians to work more effectively with their male clients. He has more than 30 publications and 50 national and international presentations, most of which are focused on men and masculinity. Dr. Englar-Carlson coedited the books *In the Room With Men: A Casebook of Therapeutic Change* and *Counseling Troubled Boys: A Guidebook for Professionals*. In 2007 he was named the Researcher of the Year by the Society for the Psychological Study of Men and Masculinity. He is also a member of the APA Working Group to Develop Guidelines for Psychological Practice With Boys and Men. As a clinician, he has worked with children, adults, and families in school, community, and university mental health settings.